LIVING THE QUESTIONS IN John

A NavStudy Featuring

D0326038

NAVPRESS®

BRINGING TRUTH TO LIFE

OUR GUARANTEE TO YOU

We believe so strongly in the message of our books that we are making this quality guarantee to you. If for any reason you are disappointed with the content of this book, return the title page to us with your name and address and we will refund to you the list price of the book. To help us serve you better, please briefly describe why you were disappointed. Mail your refund request to: NavPress, P.O. Box 35002, Colorado Springs, CO 80935.

The Navigators is an international Christian organization. Our mission is to reach, disciple, and equip people to know Christ and to make Him known through successive generations. We envision multitudes of diverse people in the United States and every other nation who have a passionate love for Christ, live a lifestyle of sharing Christ's love, and multiply spiritual laborers among those without Christ.

NavPress is the publishing ministry of The Navigators. NavPress publications help believers learn biblical truth and apply what they learn to their lives and ministries. Our mission is to stimulate spiritual formation among our readers.

ISBN 1-57683-834-X

Cover design by Disciple Design
Cover photo by Gary Walpole
Creative Team: Steve Parolini, Arvid Wallen, Cara Iverson, Pat Reinheimer

Written and compiled by John Blase

Some of the anecdotal illustrations in this book are true to life and are included with the permission of the persons involved. All other illustrations are composites of real situations, and any resemblance to people living or dead is coincidental.

All Scripture quotations in this publication are taken from *THE MESSAGE* (MSG). Copyright © 1993, 1994, 1995, 1996, 2000, 2001, 2002. Used by permission of NavPress Publishing Group.

Printed in Canada

1 2 3 4 5 6 7 8 9 10 / 09 08 07 06 05

CONTENTS

ABOUT THE
LIVING THE QUESTIONS
SERIES

I want to beg you, as much as I can . . . to be patient toward
all that is unsolved in your heart and try to love the questions
themselves like locked rooms and like books that are written
in a very foreign tongue. Do not now seek the answers, which
cannot be given you because you would not be able to live
them. . . . Live the questions now. Perhaps you will
then gradually, without noticing it, live along some
distant day into the answer.

RAINER MARIA RILKE, *LETTERS TO A YOUNG POET*

Christians usually think about Jesus as the One with all the answers;
the God-man with the evidence the verdict demands; a divine answer-
man, sent down to earth to give us just what we need. And yes, he did
give us just what we needed. Yet a careful reading of the Gospels shows
that Jesus asked just as many questions as he gave outright answers.
You would not have found a "The Bible says it, I believe it, and that
settles it" bumper sticker on Jesus' backpack. It was more like, "This is
God's Word. Stop and think about it, and let's talk about it."

However, the perception of Jesus as the divine answer-man appeals
to a great many people. Life has questions, so you go to the Scriptures,
look on the right page, find the answers, and everything's good. But
while that works great for algebra class, it just doesn't seem to work
well for this thing called *life*. Could the "divine answer-man" approach
be too simplistic? Too one-dimensional for such a deep character as
Jesus Christ? For one, it seems to leave you and me, the children of

God, out of the picture. We're not colaborers with God; we're just laborers.

Jesus went about doing good. Apparently part of this "good" was asking great questions—questions that would cause people to stop and pause and ponder the things they were living for and what might be worth dying for; questions not bound by a calendar but applicable to the ages; questions as poignant today as they were then.

The book you hold in your hand takes the approach of looking at the questions found in the Gospels—the questions Jesus asked. The questions are specific to the text of Eugene Peterson's *The Message*. I'm talking about questions such as, "All this time and money wasted on fashion—do you think it makes that much difference?" or "Who needs a doctor: the healthy or the sick?" Our temptation might be to respond quickly because we think we know the answers. But what if these questions must be lived? Lived out in dimensions such as friendship, family, and church? Lived out in locales such as homes, classrooms, and forests primeval? Lived by the flesh and blood whose main focus is the future, and lived by those who think mainly of the past? And what if living out these questions might lead us one day, gradually, without noticing it, into The Answer—the One who described himself as the way, truth, and life?

Live the questions now.

HOW TO USE THIS DISCUSSION GUIDE

1. This NavStudy is meant to be completed on your own *and* in a small group. You'll want to line up your study group ahead of time. A group of four to six is optimal—any bigger and one or more members will likely be shut out of discussions. Your small group can also be two. Each person will need his or her own copy of this book.

2. Lessons open with a Scripture passage intended to help you to prepare your heart and mind for the content that follows. Don't skip over this preparation time. Use it to reflect, slow down from a busy life, and transition into your study time.

3. *Read* the Scripture passages and other readings in each lesson. Let it all soak in. Re-read if necessary. There's no blue ribbon for finishing quickly. Make notes in the white space on the page. If you like journaling, think of this as a space to journal. If you don't like journaling, just think of it as space to "think out loud on paper."

4. *Think* about what you read. Respond to the questions we've provided. Always ask, "What does this mean?" and "Why does this matter?" about the readings. Compare different Bible translations for Scripture readings. Respond to the questions we've provided, and then discuss the questions when you're in your small group. Allow the experience of others to broaden your wisdom. You'll be stretched—called upon to evaluate what you've discovered and asked to make practical sense of it. In community, that stretching can often be painful and sometimes even embarrassing. But your willingness to be transparent—your openness to the possibility of personal growth—will reap great rewards.

5. *Pray* as you go through the entire session: before you read a word, in the middle of your thinking process, when you get stuck on a

concept or passage, and as you approach the time when you'll explore these passages and thoughts together in a small group. Pause when you need to ask God for inspiration or when you need to cry out in frustration. Compose a prayer prompted by what you've uncovered in the readings and your responses to the "Think" questions.

6. *Live.* (That's "live" as in "rhymes with give" as in "Give me something I can really use in my life.") This is a place to choose one thing you can do to live out the question posed in the lesson. Don't try to craft a plan that is lofty or unreachable. Choose something small, something doable. Then, in your small group, talk about this "one thing." Commit to following through on your idea, wrestle with what that means in practical terms, and call upon your group members to hold you accountable.

7. *Follow up.* Don't let the life application drift away without action. Be accountable to small-group members and refer to previous "Live" as in "rhymes with give" sections often. Take time at the beginning of each new study to review. See how you're doing.

SMALL-GROUP STUDY TIPS

After going through each week's study on your own, it's time to sit down with others and go deeper. Here are a few thoughts on how to make the most of your small-group discussion time.

Set ground rules. You don't need many. Here are two:

First, you'll want group members to make a commitment to the entire ten-week study. Significant personal growth happens when group members spend enough time together to really get to know each other. Hit-and-miss attendance can hinder this growth.

Second, agree together that everyone's story is important. Time is a valuable commodity, so if you have an hour to spend together, do your best to give each person ample time to express concerns, pass along insights, and generally feel like a participating member of the group. Small-group discussions are not monologues. However, a one-person-dominated discussion isn't always a bad thing. Not only is your role in a small group to explore and expand your own understanding, it's also to support one another. If someone truly needs more of the floor, give it to him or her. There will be times when the needs of the one outweigh the needs of the many. Use good judgment and allow extra space when needed. *Your* time might be next week.

Meet regularly. Choose a time and place, and stick to it. Consistency removes stress that could otherwise frustrate discussion and subsequent personal growth.

Follow the book outline. Each week, open your small-group time with prayer, and read aloud the reflective Scripture passage that opens the lesson. Then go through the study together, reading each section aloud and discussing it with your group members. Tell others what you wrote. Write down new insights gleaned from other group members. Wrestle the questions together. When you get to the "Pray" section, ask for volunteers willing to read aloud their written prayers. Finally, spend a few minutes talking together about each person's "one thing" and how to achieve that goal.

Talk openly. If you enter this study with shields up, you're probably not alone. And you're not a "bad person" for your hesitation to unpack your life in front of friends or strangers. Maybe you're skeptical about the value of revealing to others the deepest parts of who you are. Maybe you're simply too afraid of what might fall out of the suitcase. You don't have to go to a place where you're uncomfortable. If you want to sit and listen, offer a few thoughts, or even express a surface level of your own pain, go ahead. But don't neglect what brings you to this place—that longing for meaning. You can't ignore it away. Dip your feet in the water of brutally honest discussion, and you may choose to dive in. There is healing here.

Stay on task. Refrain from sharing material that falls into the "too much information" category. Don't spill unnecessary stuff. If structure isn't your group's strength, try a few minutes of general comments about the study, and then take each question one at a time and give everyone in the group a chance to respond.

"If I tell you things that are plain as the hand before your face and you don't believe me, what use is there in telling you of things you can't see, the things of God?" (John 3:12)

Before You Begin

Take some time to reflect and prepare your heart and mind for this study. Read the following Scripture passage. Soak up God's Word. There's no hurry. Then, when you're ready, turn the page and begin.

PSALM 40:9-10

I've preached you to the whole congregation,
    I've kept back nothing, GOD—you know that.
I didn't keep the news of your ways
    a secret, didn't keep it to myself.
I told it all, how dependable you are, how thorough.
    I didn't hold back pieces of love and truth
For myself alone. I told it all,
    let the congregation know the whole story.

READ

John 3:1-16

There was a man of the Pharisee sect, Nicodemus, a prominent leader among the Jews. Late one night he visited Jesus and said, "Rabbi, we all know you're a teacher straight from God. No one could do all the God-pointing, God-revealing acts you do if God weren't in on it."

Jesus said, "You're absolutely right. Take it from me: Unless a person is born from above, it's not possible to see what I'm pointing to—to God's kingdom."

"How can anyone," said Nicodemus, "be born who has already been born and grown up? You can't re-enter your mother's womb and be born again. What are you saying with this 'born-from-above' talk?"

Jesus said, "You're not listening. Let me say it again. Unless a person submits to this original creation—the 'wind hovering over the water' creation, the invisible moving the visible, a baptism into a new life—it's not possible to enter God's kingdom. When you look at a baby, it's just that: a body you can look at and touch. But the person who takes shape within is formed by something you can't see and touch—the Spirit—and becomes a living spirit.

"So don't be so surprised when I tell you that you have to be 'born from above'—out of this world, so to speak. You know well enough how the wind blows this way and that. You hear it rustling through the trees, but you have no idea where it comes from or where it's headed next. That's the way it is with everyone 'born from above' by the wind of God, the Spirit of God."

Nicodemus asked, "What do you mean by this? How does this happen?"

Jesus said, "You're a respected teacher of Israel and you don't know these basics? Listen carefully. I'm speaking sober truth to you. I speak only of what I know by experience; I give witness only to what I have seen with my own eyes. There is nothing secondhand here, no hearsay. Yet instead of facing the evidence and accepting it, you procrastinate with questions. **If I tell you things that are plain as the hand before your face and you don't believe me, what use is there in telling you of things you can't see, the things of God?**

"No one has ever gone up into the presence of God except the One who came down from that Presence, the Son of Man. In the same way that Moses lifted the serpent in the desert so people could have something to see and then believe, it is necessary for the Son of Man to be lifted up—and everyone who looks up to him, trusting and expectant, will gain a real life, eternal life.

"This is how much God loved the world: He gave his Son, his one and only Son. And this is why: so that no one need be destroyed; by believing in him, anyone can have a whole and lasting life."

THINK   "If I tell you things that are plain as the hand before your face and you don't believe me, what use is there in telling you of things you can't see, the things of God?"

- What is your immediate response to this question?
- Why do you think you responded in this way?
- Do either of the statements "born again" or "born from above" evoke any feelings in you? If so, think about where you first heard the phrase and who used it. What was your initial reaction? How does that compare to your reaction today?
- How do you feel when you read these words: "Unless a person is born from above, it's not possible to see . . . God's kingdom"?
- Make a list of what you believe to be the Christian basics.
- What is your response to Jesus' use of the word "basics" to describe things like being "born from above," "invisible moving the visible," "hear it rustling through the trees," "something you can't see and touch"? How do you think Nicodemus felt?

THINK (continued)

READ

From *Walking on Water*, by Madeleine L'Engle[1]

The well-intentioned mothers who don't want their children pol-
luted by fairy tales would not only deny them their childhood,
with its high creativity, but they would have them conform to
the secular world, with its dirty devices. The world of fairy tale,
fantasy, myth, is inimical to the secular world, and in total opposi-
tion to it, for it is interested not in limited laboratory proofs, but
in truth.

From *Orthodoxy*, by G. K. Chesterton[2]

My first and last philosophy, that which I believe in with unbroken certainty, I learnt in the nursery. I generally learnt it from
a nurse; that is, from the solemn and star-appointed priestess
at once of democracy and tradition. The things I believed most
then, the things I believe most now, are the things called fairy
tales. They seem to me to be the entirely reasonable things:
compared with them other things are fantastic. Compared with
them religion and rationalism are both abnormal, though religion
is abnormally right and rationalism abnormally wrong. Fairyland
is nothing but the sunny country of common sense. . . . I am
concerned with a certain way of looking at life, which was created
in me by the fairy tales, but has since been meekly ratified by the
mere facts.

It might be stated this way. There are certain sequences or
developments (cases of one thing following another), which are,
in the true sense of the word, reasonable. They are, in the true
sense of the word, necessary. Such are the mathematical and
merely logical sequences. We in fairyland (who are the most reasonable of all creatures) admit that reason and that necessity. For
instance, if the Ugly Sisters are older than Cinderella, it is (in an
iron and awful sense) necessary that Cinderella is younger than
the Ugly Sisters. There is no getting out of it. . . . If Jack is the son
of a miller, a miller is the father of Jack. Cold reason decrees it

from her awful throne: and we in fairyland submit. If the three brothers all ride horses, there are six animals and eighteen legs involved: that is true rationalism, and fairyland is full of it. But as I put my head over the hedge of the elves and began to take notice of the natural world, I observed extraordinary things. I observed that learned men in spectacles were talking of the actual things that happened—dawn and death and so on—as if they were rational and inevitable. They talked as if the fact that trees bear fruit were just as necessary as the fact that two and one trees make three. But it is not. There is an enormous difference by the test of fairyland: which is the test of the imagination. You cannot imagine two and one not making three. But you can easily imagine trees not growing fruit; you can imagine them growing golden candlesticks or tigers hanging on by the tail.

THINK

"If I tell you things that are plain as the hand before your face and you don't believe me, what use is there in telling you of things you can't see, the things of God?"

- What is your initial reaction to these excerpts? Why do you think these excerpts were the ones chosen to be represented in an exploration of things that are "plain as the hand before your face" and "things you can't see"?
- Were fairy tales and myths a part of your childhood? If so, what were your favorites and why?
- What do these excerpts suggest about the role of "belief" in fairy tales and myths? Can you apply that understanding of belief to faith? Why or why not?
- How does your belief relate to "things you can't see, the things of God"?

THINK (continued)

READ

From *Amazing Grace*, Kathleen Norris[3]

I find it sad to consider that belief has become a scary word, because at its Greek root, "to believe" simply means "to give one's heart to." Thus, if we can determine what it is we give our heart to, then we will know what it is to believe.

But the word "belief" has been impoverished; it has come to mean a head-over-heart intellectual assent. When people ask, "What do you believe?" they are usually asking, "What do you think?" I have come to see that my education, even my religious education, left me with a faulty and inadequate sense of religious belief as a kind of suspension of the intellect. Religion, as I came to understand it, was a primitive relic that could not stand up to the advances made in our understanding of human psychological development or the inquiry of higher mathematics and the modern sciences.

Yet I knew religious people who were psychologists, mathematicians, and scientists. So I had to assume that religious belief was simply beyond my grasp. Other people had it, I did not. And for a long time, even though I was attracted to church, I was convinced that I did not belong there, because my beliefs were not thoroughly solid, set in stone.

When I first stumbled upon the Benedictine Abbey where I am now an oblate, I was surprised to find the monks so unconcerned with my weighty doubts and intellectual frustrations over Christianity. What interested them more was my desire to come to their worship, the liturgy of the hours. I was a bit disappointed—I had thought that my doubts were spectacular obstacles to my faith and was confused but intrigued when an old monk blithely stated that doubt is merely the seed of faith, a sign that faith is alive and ready to grow. I am grateful now for his wisdom and grateful to the community for teaching me about the power of liturgy. They seemed to believe that if I just kept coming back to worship, kept coming home, things would eventually fall into place.

THINK
"If I tell you things that are plain as the hand before your face and you don't believe me, what use is there in telling you of things you can't see, the things of God?"

- What do you feel after reading Norris's words?
- "Doubt is merely the seed of faith." If you spoke that sentence in your next church group meeting, what kind of a response do you think you would get?
- How can "things that are plain as the hand before your face" lead you to belief in "things you can't see"? Is this what Norris is suggesting?
- What are some of the things you experience that can help things "fall into place" regarding your faith?

READ

From *The Orphean Passages*, by Walter Wangerin Jr.[4]

There came the Sunday which was not unlike a thousand other Sundays, a thousand earlier worships, stretching backward as far as the boy could remember, but to which the boy now paid attention as he never had before.

They went to church. Orpheus was quiet, as though a voice said, "Listen! You will hear something today." And, "Watch! You will see something today." In fact, there was no voice; but there was in him a keen awareness and anticipation.

The words of worship droned. The talking was opaque to him, sounds of various pitches and intensities, signifying little; he could not enter the talking.

He liked the singing because he'd always liked to sing. That was satisfying.

But then an awesome drama began to be enacted. People got up and began to move about the room with such solemnity that Orpheus sensed a meaning here, and he felt a twitch of fear. Moreover, everyone except himself seemed to know both the moves and their significance: he was somewhat alien. Now, this dreadfulness of the moment, and his shrinking in humility before it, were feelings familiar to him; this was experience on a higher plane; the Unknown Other was more nearly active than usual and in control. Orpheus, sensing this, got up on his knees in the pew and shot his eyes about the room, trying to see as much of this drama as he could, but afraid. Something was going to happen.

Suddenly it became very personal. His own mother got up and left his side. With her head bowed and her hands folded, she joined a line of people that stretched to the front of this vast room. Step by step, in a slow dance, she went forward. One by one she climbed steps into a raised and Sacred Place; men, dressed in long robes, bowed to her; she bowed back, and kneeled down before them: she had been admitted into a Presence. Orpheus, his heart ramming, craned his neck to see.

What were they going to do to his mother?

Now one of these robed men approached his mother, putting his face very close to hers, and his hand to her mouth, a gesture so intimate between the two that Orpheus felt ashamed to see it. And the man mumbled to her, and she nodded; and when he left her, she was chewing. He had given her something to swallow. Why would he feed her? Why would she allow him to treat her like a baby? He hurt for his mother, so weak, so weak upon her knees. No, this was different from the mother he knew.

And then another man came to her and put an enormous cup to her lips, and she drank from it, and she did not argue. Then she bowed her head so deep that it disappeared below her shoulders, and Orpheus had the sudden grisly impression that the head of his mother was gone. . . .

She rose; she turned; she traveled the long aisle back to him. She smiled at him. . . . She sat beside him and bowed her head and began to pray.

And then he smelled the smell.

His mother moved in a cloud. There flowed from her nose a scent both sweet and penetrating, new and altogether mystic. When he breathed it in, it seemed to suffuse his whole being. It was wonderful. It made his mother wonderful. He gazed at her while she prayed.

He touched her shoulder.

"Mama," he whispered. "What did you eat?"

"A piece of bread," she said, and he smelled the smell more strongly still.

He made strange eyes at her. Not bread. Bread didn't fill the drama. Really? Was it only bread?

She looked a moment on him, then spoke seriously. "I ate the body of Jesus," she said.

Orpheus knew the truth by experience, that when the Other was in control, then no reality could be taken for granted; all realities could melt into other realities; neither names nor habits could keep things as they were. Therefore, that a piece of bread should be a bit of someone's body didn't seem impossible to him. He accepted that.

His mother said, "And I drank his blood."

Solemnly, solemnly Orpheus nodded back to her. Blood. Blood was a strange and terrible thing to drink. It poured from wounds and pain. . . . It was life. Blood fit the undefined enormity of the drama. The Other was near indeed. The Other was very close to Orpheus now, because it had also seized on his own mother, shattering her common reality, making her to do and then to speak impossible things: "I drank his blood"—and then to smile upon him, Orpheus, her son.

Orpheus whispered, "Is that what I smell?" If he could smell it, then he had been admitted into mystery.

She said, "Yes."

He said, "Whose blood Mama?"

And she said, "The blood of Jesus."

Jesus.

THINK   "If I tell you things that are plain as the hand before your face and you don't believe me, what use is there in telling you of things you can't see, the things of God?"

- In what way is this story a picture of something as "plain as the hand before your face"? In what way is it a picture of "things you can't see"?
- Is there any similarity in *this* story of entering "mystery" and your own story? Describe those similarities, and then list the differences.
- What does Orpheus's story teach you about how God can work to help people discover the things of God? What does your own faith conversion story tell you?

THINK (continued)

READ

From *Traveling Mercies*, by Anne Lamott[5]

I went back to St. Andrew about once a month. No one tried
to con me into sitting down or staying. I always left before the
sermon. I loved singing, even about Jesus, but I just didn't want
to be preached at about him. To me, Jesus made about as much
sense as Scientology or dowsing. But the church smelled wonderful, like the air had nourishment in it, or like it was composed
of these people's exhalations, of warmth and faith and peace.
There were always children running around or being embraced,
and a gorgeous stick-thin deaf black girl signing to her mother,
hearing the songs and the Scripture through her mother's flash-
ing fingers. The radical old women of the congregation were
famous in those parts for having convinced the very conservative
national Presbytery to donate ten thousand dollars to the Angela
Davis Defense fund during her trial up at the Civic Center. And
every other week they brought huge tubs of great food for the
homeless families living at the shelter near the canal to the north.
I loved this. But it was the singing that pulled me in and split me
wide open.

That April of 1984, in the midst of this experience, Pammy
took a fourth urine sample to the lab, and it finally came back
positive. I had published three books by then, but none of
them had sold particularly well, and I did not have the money
or wherewithal to have a baby. The father was someone I had
just met, who was married, and no one I wanted a real life or
baby with. So Pammy one evening took me in for the abortion,
and I was sadder than I'd been since my father died, and when
she brought me home that night, I went upstairs to my loft . . .
and . . . drank until nearly dawn. . . . On the seventh night,
though, very drunk and just about to take a sleeping pill, I discovered that I was bleeding heavily. It did not stop over the next
hour. . . . I got in bed, shaky and sad and too wild to have another
drink or take a sleeping pill. I had a cigarette and turned off the

light. After a while, as I lay there, I became aware of someone with me, hunkered down in the corner, and I just assumed it was my father, whose presence I had felt over the years when I was frightened and alone. The feeling was so strong that I actually turned on the light for a moment to make sure no one was there—of course, there wasn't. But after a while, in the dark again, I knew beyond any doubt that it was Jesus. I felt him as surely as I feel my dog lying nearby as I write this.

And I was appalled. I thought about my life and my brilliant hilarious progressive friends, I thought about what everyone would think of me if I became a Christian, and it seemed an utterly impossible thing that simply could not be allowed to happen. I turned to the wall and said out loud, "I would rather die."

I felt him sitting there on his haunches in the corner of my sleeping loft, watching me with patience and love, and I squinched my eyes shut, but that didn't help because that's not what I was seeing him with.

Finally I fell asleep, and in the morning, he was gone.

This experience spooked me badly, but I thought it was just an apparition, born of fear and self-loathing and booze and loss of blood. But then everywhere I went, I had the feeling that a little cat was following me, wanting me to reach down and pick it up, wanting me to open the door and let it in. But I knew what would happen: you let a cat in one time, give it a little milk, and then it stays forever. So I tried to keep one step ahead of it, slamming my houseboat door when I entered or left.

And one week later, when I went back to church, I was so hungover that I couldn't stand up for the songs, and this time I stayed for the sermon, which I just thought was so ridiculous, like someone trying to convince me of the existence of extra-terrestrials, but the last song was so deep and raw and pure that I could not escape. It was as if the people were singing in between the notes, weeping and joyful at the same time, and I felt like their voices or something was rocking me in its bosom, holding me like a scared kid, and I opened up to that feeling—and it washed over me.

I began to cry and left before the benediction, and I raced home and felt the little cat running along at my heels, and I walked down the dock past dozens of potted flowers, under a sky as blue as one of God's own dreams, and I opened the door to my houseboat, and I stood there a minute, and then I hung my head and said, ". . . All right. You can come in."

So this was my beautiful moment of conversion.

THINK   "If I tell you things that are plain as the hand before your face and you don't believe me, what use is there in telling you of things you can't see, the things of God?"

- What is your initial reaction to Anne's story? Why do you think you reacted that way?
- What are examples of "things you can't see, the things of God" in Anne's story? Why do you think she fought against these?
- Where do you find these things in your own life? Have you also fought against them, not wanting to "let the cat in"? Explain.

PRAY

Look back at the "Think" sections. Ruminate on your responses. Let them distill into a prayer, and then write that prayer below.

Author of my story . . .

The issue of prayer is not prayer; the issue of prayer is God.

ABRAHAM HESCHEL

LIVE

"If I tell you things that are plain as the hand before your face and you don't believe me, what use is there in telling you of things you can't see, the things of God?"

The challenge now is to take this question further along—to live out this question. Think of one thing, *just one*, that you can personally do to wrestle with the question, inhabit the character of it, and live it in everyday life. In the following space, jot down your thoughts on this "one thing." Read the Scripture and quotes that follow for additional inspiration. During the coming week, pray about this "one thing," talk with a close friend about it, and learn to live the question.

One thing . . .

Religion is the fashionable substitute for belief.

Oscar Wilde

As you read over what I have written to you, you'll be able to see for yourselves into the mystery of Christ. None of our ancestors understood this. Only in our time has it been made clear by God's Spirit through his holy apostles and prophets of this new order. The mystery is that people who have never heard of God and those who have heard of him all their lives (what I've been calling outsiders and insiders) stand on the same ground before God. They get the same offer, same help, same promises in Christ Jesus. The Message is accessible and welcoming to everyone, across the board.

Ephesians 3:4-6

Live the questions now. Perhaps you will then gradually, without noticing it, live along some distant day into the answer.

RAINER MARIA RILKE, *LETTERS TO A YOUNG POET*

"Would you give me a drink of water?"
(John 4:7)

Before You Begin

Take some time to reflect and prepare your heart and mind for this study. Read the following Scripture passage. Soak up God's Word. There's no hurry. Then, when you're ready, turn the page and begin.

JOHN 4:13-14

Jesus said, "Everyone who drinks this water will get thirsty again and again. Anyone who drinks the water I give will never thirst—not ever. The water I give will be an artesian spring within, gushing fountains of endless life."

READ

John 4:1-26

Jesus realized that the Pharisees were keeping count of the baptisms that he and John performed (although his disciples, not Jesus, did the actual baptizing). They had posted the score that Jesus was ahead, turning him and John into rivals in the eyes of the people. So Jesus left the Judean countryside and went back to Galilee.

To get there, he had to pass through Samaria. He came into Sychar, a Samaritan village that bordered the field Jacob had given his son Joseph. Jacob's well was still there. Jesus, worn out by the trip, sat down at the well. It was noon.

A woman, a Samaritan, came to draw water. Jesus said, **"Would you give me a drink of water?"** (His disciples had gone to the village to buy food for lunch.)

The Samaritan woman, taken aback, asked, "How come you, a Jew, are asking me, a Samaritan woman, for a drink?" (Jews in those days wouldn't be caught dead talking to Samaritans.)

Jesus answered, "If you knew the generosity of God and who I am, you would be asking *me* for a drink, and I would give you fresh, living water."

The woman said, "Sir, you don't even have a bucket to draw with, and this well is deep. So how are you going to get this 'living water'? Are you a better man than our ancestor Jacob, who dug this well and drank from it, he and his sons and livestock, and passed it down to us?"

Jesus said, "Everyone who drinks this water will get thirsty again and again. Anyone who drinks the water I give will never thirst—not ever. The water I give will be an artesian spring within, gushing fountains of endless life."

The woman said, "Sir, give me this water so I won't ever get thirsty, won't ever have to come back to this well again!"

He said, "Go call your husband and then come back."

"I have no husband," she said.

"That's nicely put: 'I have no husband.' You've had five husbands, and the man you're living with now isn't even your husband. You spoke the truth there, sure enough."

"Oh, so you're a prophet! Well, tell me this: Our ancestors worshiped God at this mountain, but you Jews insist that Jerusalem is the only place for worship, right?"

"Believe me, woman, the time is coming when you Samaritans will worship the Father neither here at this mountain nor there in Jerusalem. You worship guessing in the dark; we Jews worship in the clear light of day. God's way of salvation is made available through the Jews. But the time is coming—it has, in fact, come—when what you're called will not matter and where you go to worship will not matter.

"It's who you are and the way you live that count before God. Your worship must engage your spirit in the pursuit of truth. That's the kind of people the Father is out looking for: those who are simply and honestly *themselves* before him in their worship. God is sheer being itself—Spirit. Those who worship him must do it out of their very being, their spirits, their true selves, in adoration."

The woman said, "I don't know about that. I do know that the Messiah is coming. When he arrives, we'll get the whole story."

"I am he," said Jesus. "You don't have to wait any longer or look any further."

THINK   *"Would you give me a drink of water?"*

- What is your immediate response to this question?
- Why do you think you responded in this way?
- Verse 4 reads that Jesus "had to pass through Samaria." Think about a time when you had to pass through unfriendly territory. Hint: This is a place (literal or figurative) where you usually wouldn't be caught dead.
- What do you think of Jesus' question "Would you give me a drink?"

- Did you end up talking to anyone in your Samaria-like place? If so, did you initiate conversation, or did someone else?
- How did you feel during the conversation? How did it go?
- Why do you think you had to pass through that place?

READ

From *Of Wolves and Men*, by Barry Lopez[1]

I think, as the twentieth century comes to a close, that we are coming to an understanding of animals different from the one that has guided us for the past three hundred years. We have begun to see again, as our primitive ancestors did, that animals are neither imperfect imitations of men nor machines that can be described entirely in terms of endocrine secretions and neural impulses. Like us, they are genetically variable, and both the species and the individual are capable of unprecedented behavior. . . .

I do not think it possible to define completely the sort of animals men require in order to live. They are always changing and are different for different peoples. Nor do I think it possible that science can by itself produce the animal entire. The range of the human mind, the scale and depth of the metaphors the mind is capable of manufacturing as it grapples with the universe, stand in stunning contrast to the belief that there is only one reality, which is man's, or worse, that only one culture among the many on earth possesses the truth.

To allow mystery, which is to say to yourself, "There could be more, there could be things we don't understand," is not to damn knowledge. It is to take a wider view. It is to permit yourself an extraordinary freedom: someone else does not have to be wrong in order that you may be right.

In the Western world, in the biological sciences, we have an extraordinary tool for discovery of knowledge about animals, together with a system for its classification; and through the existence of journals and libraries we have a system for its dissemination. But if we are going to learn more about animals—real knowledge, not more facts—we are going to have to get out into the woods.

THINK   "Would you give me a drink of water?"

- Later in the book, Lopez uses the wolf as a symbol of that which many people are scared of and would like to see eradicated. However, their understanding of the wolf is limited at best, and they are totally ignorant at worst. The Samaritan people held a similar place in the eyes of most Jews. They were wild half-breeds, and the world would be much better off without them. Who are some individuals or groups of people that you have those kinds of opinions about?

- "But if we are going to learn more . . . we are going to have to get out into the woods." What kinds of thoughts and feelings does this sentence evoke in you? What would "the woods" mean in your life?

- Have you had any experiences where "time in the woods" changed your perspective on a group or an individual? Be as detailed as possible.

READ

From *Living Toward a Vision*, by Walter Brueggemann[2]

If you ask almost any adult about the impact of church school on his or her growth, he or she will not tell you about books or curriculum or Bible stories or anything like that. The central memory is of the teacher, learning is *meeting*. That poses problems for the characteristically American way of thinking about education for competence even in the church. Meeting never made anybody competent. Surely we need competence, unless we mean to dismantle much of our made world. But our business is not competence. It is meeting. We are learning slowly and late that *education for competence* without *education as meeting* promises us deadly values and scary options. And anyway, one can't become "competent" in morality or in Bible stories. But one can have life-changing meetings that open one to new kinds of existence. And that surely is what church education must be about. . . . Our penchant for control and predictability, our commitment to quantity, our pursuit of stability and security—all this gives us a sense of priority and an agenda that is concerned to reduce the element of surprise and newness in our lives. And when newness and surprise fail, there is not likely to be graciousness, healing, or joy. Enough critics have made the point that when experiences of surprise and newness are silenced in our lives, there is no amazement, and where there is no amazement, there cannot be the full coming to health, wholeness, and maturity.

THINK "Would you give me a drink of water?"

- What is your first response to Brueggemann's words?
- Who were some of your teachers who exemplified "learning is meeting"?
- Think about the progression here. We're moving into Samaritan territory, or the woods, with the goal of learning, but this learning is not necessarily to be equated with competence.

We're not talking about being competent around Samaritans or wolves; we're talking about *meeting* them. It is a totally unpredictable quest that can lead to things such as "health, wholeness, and maturity." What is your response to this progression?

READ

From *The Memory of Old Jack*, by Wendell Berry[3]

In buying that Farrier place he had destroyed his old independence. He had more to do now than he could do alone. Uncle Henry was still there, of course, as he would be until he died. But Uncle Henry had already been old a long time, and he would not be able for long to do the little that he still did. Jack needed a good hand, and after some looking around, he hired a young Negro man who had been recommended to him by Perry Clemmons. This was a strongly built, very dark man, whose eyes had a straight, calm look that Jack liked. He had a wife, Marthy, lighter in color than himself, and four children. He was said to be a good worker, a quiet man, one who could be depended on. His name was Will Wells.

There was on the Farrier place a small house of two rooms, long disused, and this they repaired for Will and his family, who moved in at the end of the second week of March. Will lived up to the good that had been said of him, and more. He would get out early and stay late. He would work responsibly alone. He took an intelligent pride in what he did, and was able to see what needed to be done and to do it without being told. He was a good man with stock and a competent teamster. He was perhaps four or five years younger than Jack, strong, proud of his strength, eager in its use.

There grew between the two of them a relationship—a sort of brotherhood—of an intensity that Jack would know only that once. Though they assumed the inevitable economic roles of master and servant, they were from the beginning equals before the work. It would not have occurred to Jack to ask another man to do a job that he would not do himself, or to hold back while another man worked. That was his principle and his pride. Though Will worked for Jack's benefit, he did not work for his convenience. That they worked side by side, that they knew the same hardships of labor and weather, made a ground of respect between them, and a liking. They teamed together as if they had been born twins. Both were big men, both strong, both liked the work. And in the time they were together they did an amount of it that amazed both themselves and the men who knew them. They acquired a local fame as a team among the farmers who worked with them in the tobacco setting and in the harvest. When the two of them stepped up, other men stood back.

Little idle talk ever passed between them. They might work closely together for half a day without speaking, cooperating like the two hands of a single body, anticipating each other's moves like partners in a dance. They did not speak of their lives. They met and did their work and parted and went their ways. They met in Port William as awkwardly as strangers. It was in the work itself, not in anything that the work came from or led to, that they made the terms and the comfort of their comradeship. At times in the heat and striving of some hard day their eyes would meet and acknowledge the strange grace of their labor.

THINK   "Would you give me a drink of water?"

- What do you feel after reading this passage?
- Have you ever had an experience like Jack's—where someone totally different from you came alongside you and, if for even a short time, you experienced a "strange grace"?
- Later on in the story, the relationship between the two begins to deteriorate. Berry describes the heart of this time: "There came between them in the third year . . . a disharmony, a withdrawal from the center of their agreement. . . . In Will this was the result of a failure of interest that had been imminent all along in his knowledge that his labor formalized and preserved no bond between him and the place; he was a man laboring for no more than his existence." How is this like or unlike something you've experienced?

• Think again about the woman at the well—a woman laboring for no more than her existence. Do you see any differences between how Jesus related to this woman and how Jack related to Will? What are those differences? What do they say to you about how to live out what it means to give someone "a drink of water"?

PRAY

Look back at the "Think" sections. Ruminate on your responses. Let them distill into a prayer, and then write that prayer below.

Here I am, Lord, send me . . .

The issue of prayer is not prayer; the issue of prayer is God.

ABRAHAM HESCHEL

LIVE

"Would you give me a drink of water?"

The challenge now is to take this question further along—to live out this question. Think of one thing, *just one*, that you can personally do to wrestle with the question, inhabit the character of it, and live it in everyday life. In the following space, jot down your thoughts on this "one thing." Read the Scripture and quotes that follow for additional inspiration. During the coming week, pray about this "one thing," talk with a close friend about it, and learn to live the question.

One thing...

I don't think that it is always necessary to talk *about* the deepest and most private dimension of who we are, but I think we are called to talk to each other *out of* it, and just as importantly to listen to each other out of it, to live out of our depths as well as our shadows.

Frederick Buechner

"Then the King will say to those on his right, 'Enter, you who are blessed by my Father! Take what's coming to you in this kingdom. It's been ready for you since the world's foundation. And here's why:

I was hungry and you fed me,
I was thirsty and you gave me a drink,
I was homeless and you gave me a room,
I was shivering and you gave me clothes,
I was sick and you stopped to visit,
I was in prison and you came to me.'

"Then those 'sheep' are going to say, 'Master, what are you talking about? When did we ever see you hungry and feed you, thirsty and give you a drink? And when did we ever see you sick or in prison and come to you?' Then the King will say, 'I'm telling the solemn truth: Whenever you did one of these things to someone overlooked or ignored, that was me — you did it to me.'"

Matthew 25:34-40

Live the questions now. Perhaps you will then gradually, without noticing it, live along some distant day into the answer.

RAINER MARIA RILKE, *LETTERS TO A YOUNG POET*

LESSON 3

"Do you want to get well?"
(John 5:6)

Before You Begin

Take some time to reflect and prepare your heart and mind for this study. Read the following Scripture passage. Soak up God's Word. There's no hurry. Then, when you're ready, turn the page and begin.

MATTHEW 7:7-11

"Don't bargain with God. Be direct. Ask for what you need. This isn't a cat-and-mouse, hide-and-seek game we're in. If your child asks for bread, do you trick him with sawdust? If he asks for fish, do you scare him with a live snake on his plate? As bad as you are, you wouldn't think of such a thing. You're at least decent to your own children. So don't you think the God who conceived you in love will be even better?"

READ

John 5:1-18

Soon another Feast came around and Jesus was back in Jerusalem. Near the Sheep Gate in Jerusalem there was a pool, in Hebrew called *Bethesda*, with five alcoves. Hundreds of sick people—blind, crippled, paralyzed—were in these alcoves. One man had been an invalid there for thirty-eight years. When Jesus saw him stretched out by the pool and knew how long he had been there, he said, "**Do you want to get well?**"

The sick man said, "Sir, when the water is stirred, I don't have anybody to put me in the pool. By the time I get there, somebody else is already in."

Jesus said, "Get up, take your bedroll, start walking." The man was healed on the spot. He picked up his bedroll and walked off.

That day happened to be the Sabbath. The Jews stopped the healed man and said, "It's the Sabbath. You can't carry your bedroll around. It's against the rules."

But he told them, "The man who made me well told me to. He said, 'Take your bedroll and start walking.'"

They asked, "Who gave you the order to take it up and start walking?" But the healed man didn't know, for Jesus had slipped away into the crowd.

A little later Jesus found him in the Temple and said, "You look wonderful! You're well! Don't return to a sinning life or something worse might happen."

The man went back and told the Jews that it was Jesus who had made him well. That is why the Jews were out to get Jesus—because he did this kind of thing on the Sabbath.

But Jesus defended himself. "My Father is working straight through, even on the Sabbath. So am I."

That really set them off. The Jews were now not only out to expose him; they were out to *kill* him. Not only was he breaking the Sabbath, but he was calling God his own Father, putting himself on a level with God.

THINK   "Do you want to get well?"

- What is your immediate response to this question?
- Why do you think you responded in this way?
- There were hundreds of sick people tucked away in the alcoves, waiting for an angelic stirring of the waters, and all their hopes rested in getting in that water quickly. But this man had no one to help him in the race for the cure. Even though the man had been an invalid for thirty-eight years, Jesus asked him if he wanted to get well. How do you think the man felt when he was singled out for this?
- What would have been your response to Jesus' question? Would your optimism be strong, or would you be more cynical and resigned?

READ

From *Walking on Water*, by Madeleine L'Engle[1]

Kairos. Real time. God's time. That time which breaks through chronos with a shock of joy, that time we do not recognize while we are expecting it, but only afterwards, because kairos has nothing to do with chronological time. In kairos we are completely unselfconscious, and yet paradoxically far more real than we can ever be when we are constantly checking our watches for chronological time. The saint, in contemplation, lost (discovered) to self in the mind of God is in kairos. The artist at work is in kairos. The child at play, totally thrown outside himself in the game, be it building a sandcastle or making a daisy chain, is in kairos. In kairos we become what we are called to be as human beings, co-creators with God, touching on the wonder of creation. This calling should not be limited to artists—or saints—but it is a fearful calling. Mana, taboo. It can destroy as well as bring into being. . . .

Freedom is a terrible gift, and the theory behind all dictatorships is that "the people" do not want freedom. They want bread and circuses. They want workman's compensation and fringe benefits and T.V. Give up your free will, give up your freedom to make choices, listen to the expert, and you will have three cars in the garage, steak on your table, and you will no longer have to suffer the agony of choice.

Choice is an essential ingredient of fiction and drama. A protagonist must not simply be acted upon, he must act, by making a choice, a decision to do this rather than that. A series of mistaken choices throughout the centuries has brought us to a restricted way of life in which we have less freedom than we are meant to have, and so we have a sense of powerlessness and frustration which comes from our inability to change the many terrible things happening on our planet.

All the Faust stories are studies in the results of choice. Dostoevsky's story of the Grand Inquisitor in *The Brothers Karamazov* is one of the most brilliant pieces of Christian writing I know, and one of the most frightening, because the Grand Inquisitor, like many dictators, is plausible; he wants people to be happy; he does not want them to suffer; the Church, because of the great love it has for humanity, has done its best to reverse all the damage caused by Jesus, with his terrible promise of the truth that will make us free. We do not want to be free, the Grand Inquisitor assures Jesus. We want these stones to be turned into bread.

THINK   "Do you want to get well?"

- Go back and apply the kairos/chronos distinctions to the passage from John 5 (the first "Read" section in this lesson). Jesus reset the man's clock to kairos time, real time, God's time. L'Engle writes, "In kairos we become what we are called to be as human beings, co-creators with God." The man in John 5 did his part (getting up and walking) in co-creating with God a wonder of creation. Do you agree with that kind of thinking? Do you have a part to play in what God is doing? Do you believe the man had the freedom to say no to Jesus?
- "It can destroy as well as bring into being." What were some things that were destroyed in the man's life?
- How hard would it be to leave behind all you'd known for thirty-eight years? Your residence, your identity, your community, your routine?
- Do people really want freedom? Do *you*?

READ

From *The Brothers Karamazov*, by Fyodor Dostoevsky[2]

Judge Thyself who was right—Thou or he who questioned Thee then? Remember the first question; its meaning, in other words, was this: "Thou wouldst go into the world, and art going with empty hands, with some promise of freedom which men in their simplicity and their natural unruliness cannot even understand, which they fear and dread—for nothing has ever been more insupportable for a man and a human society than freedom. But seest Thou these stones in this parched and barren wilderness? Turn them into bread, and mankind will run after Thee like a flock of sheep, grateful and obedient, though for ever trembling, lest Thou withdraw Thy hand and deny them Thy bread." But Thou wouldst not deprive man of freedom and didst reject the offer, thinking, what is that freedom worth, if obedience is bought with bread? Thou didst reply that man lives not by bread alone. But dost Thou know that for the sake of that earthly bread the spirit of the earth will rise up against Thee and will strive with Thee and overcome Thee, and all will follow him, crying, "Who can compare with this beast? He has given us fire from heaven!" Dost Thou know that the ages will pass, and humanity will proclaim by the lips of their sages that there is no crime, and therefore no sin; there is only hunger? "Feed men, and then ask of them virtue!" that's what they'll write on the banner, which they will raise against Thee, and with which they will destroy Thy temple. Where Thy temple stood will rise a new building; the terrible tower of Babel will be built again, and though, like the one of old, it will not be finished, yet Thou mightest have prevented that new tower and have cut short the sufferings of men for a thousand years; for they will come back to us after a thousand years of agony with their tower. They will seek us again, hidden underground in the catacombs, for we shall be again persecuted and tortured. They will find us and cry to us, "Feed us, for those who have promised us fire from heaven haven't given it!" And then we shall finish building their tower, for he finishes the building who feeds them. And we alone shall feed them in Thy name, declaring falsely that it is in Thy name. Oh, never, never can they feed themselves without us! No science will give them bread so long as they remain free. In the end they will lay their freedom at our feet, and say to us, "Make us your slaves, but feed us." They will understand themselves, at last, that freedom and bread enough for all are inconceivable together, for never, never will they be able to share between them! They will be convinced, too, that they can never be free, for they are weak, vicious, worthless and rebellious.

Receiving bread from us, they will see clearly that we take the bread made by their hands from them, to give it to them, without any miracle. They will see that we do not change the stones to bread, but in truth they will be more thankful for taking it from our hands than for the bread itself! For they will remember only too well that in old days, without our help, even the bread they made turned to stones in their hands, while since they have come back to us, the very stones have turned to bread in their hands. Too, too well they know the value of complete submission! And until men know that, they will be unhappy. Who is most to blame for their not knowing it, speak? Who scattered the flock and sent it astray on unknown paths? But the flock will come together again and will submit once more, and then it will be once for all. Then we shall give them the quiet humble happiness of weak creatures such as they are by nature. Oh, we shall persuade them at last not to be proud, for Thou didst lift them up and thereby taught them to be proud. We shall show them that they are weak, that they are only pitiful children, but that childlike happiness is the sweetest of all. They will become timid and will look to us and huddle close to us in fear, as chicks to the hen. They will marvel at us and will be awe-stricken before us, and will be proud at our being so powerful and clever, that we have been able to subdue such a turbulent flock of thousands of millions. They will tremble impotently before our wrath, their minds will grow fearful, they will be quick to shed tears like women and children, but they will be just as ready at a sign from us to pass to laughter and rejoicing, to happy mirth and childish song. Yes, we shall set them to work, but in their leisure hours we shall make their life like a child's game, with children's songs and innocent dance. Oh, we shall allow them even sin, they are weak and helpless, and they will love us like children because we allow them to sin. We shall tell them that every sin will be expiated, if it is done with our permission, that we allow them to sin because we love them, and the punishment for these sins we take upon ourselves. And we shall take it upon ourselves, and they will adore us as their saviours who have taken on themselves their sins before God. And they will have no secrets from us. We shall allow or forbid them to live with their wives and mistresses, to have or not to have children—according to whether they have been obedient or disobedient—and they will submit to us gladly and cheerfully. The most painful secrets of their conscience, all, all they will bring to us, and we shall have an answer for all. And they will be glad to believe our answer, for it will save them from the great anxiety and terrible agony they endure at present in making a free decision for themselves. And all will be happy, all the millions of creatures except the hundred thousand who rule over them. For only we, we who guard the mystery, shall be unhappy.

There will be thousands of millions of happy babes, and a hundred thousand sufferers who have taken upon themselves the curse of the knowledge of good and evil. Peacefully they will die, peacefully they will expire in Thy name, and beyond the grave they will find nothing but death. But we shall keep the secret, and for their happiness we shall allure them with the reward of heaven and eternity. Though if there were anything in the other world, it certainly would not be for such as they.

THINK "Do you want to get well?"

- This passage is explaining what might have happened had Jesus returned to earth during the Spanish Inquisition in the sixteenth century. It is essentially a picture of the church getting along "just fine" without Jesus. What phrases in the passage caught your eye?
- Have you given up your choice to the church? To an authority figure? To a group of friends? Have you completely submitted yourself to someone in an unhealthy way? Explain your answer.
- How might people who have completely submitted themselves to an authority answer Jesus' question "Do you want to get well?" Would they even recognize that they are "sick"? Explain.

READ

Psalm 91:14-16

> "If you'll hold on to me for dear life," says GOD,
>> "I'll get you out of any trouble.
> I'll give you the best of care
>> if you'll only get to know and trust me.
> Call me and I'll answer, be at your side in bad times;
>> I'll rescue you, then throw you a party.
> I'll give you a long life,
>> give you a long drink of salvation!"

THINK   "Do you want to get well?"

- What role does trust play in allowing God to make us well?
- Is it easy to trust God to "rescue" us? Why or why not?
- If the answer to "Do you want to get well?" seems obvious but getting well isn't so easy to actually do, how can learning to trust God help you live that question?

PRAY

Look back at the "Think" sections. Ruminate on your responses.
Let them distill into a prayer, and then write that prayer below.

I want . . .

The issue of prayer is not prayer; the issue of prayer is God.

ABRAHAM HESCHEL

LIVING THE QUESTIONS SERIES

LIVE   "Do you want to get well?"

The challenge now is to take this question further along—to live out this question. Think of one thing, *just one*, that you can personally do to wrestle with the question, inhabit the character of it, and live it in everyday life. In the following space, jot down your thoughts on this "one thing." Read the Scripture and quotes that follow for additional inspiration. During the coming week, pray about this "one thing," talk with a close friend about it, and learn to live the question.

One thing . . .

Just then a woman who had hemorrhaged for twelve years slipped in from behind and lightly touched his robe. She was thinking to herself, "If I can just put a finger on his robe, I'll get well." Jesus turned—caught her at it. Then he reassured her: "Courage, daughter. You took a risk of faith, and now you're well." The woman was well from then on.

Matthew 9:20-22

Diverse are the ways by which men come to Christ. And great is the temptation to judge others if they do not have mud put on their eyes and go to Siloam exactly as we did.

Vance Havner

Live the questions now. Perhaps you will then gradually, without noticing it, live along some distant day into the answer.
RAINER MARIA RILKE, *LETTERS TO A YOUNG POET*

"Does no one condemn you?"
(John 8:10)

Before You Begin

Take some time to reflect and prepare your heart and mind for this study. Read the following Scripture passage. Soak up God's Word. There's no hurry. Then, when you're ready, turn the page and begin.

ROMANS 8:12-14

So don't you see that we don't owe this old do-it-yourself life one red cent. There's nothing in it for us, nothing at all. The best thing to do is give it a decent burial and get on with your new life. God's Spirit beckons. There are things to do and places to go!

READ

John 7:37–8:11

On the final and climactic day of the Feast, Jesus took his stand. He cried out, "If anyone thirsts, let him come to me and drink. Rivers of living water will brim and spill out of the depths of anyone who believes in me this way, just as the Scripture says." (He said this in regard to the Spirit, whom those who believed in him were about to receive. The Spirit had not yet been given because Jesus had not yet been glorified.)

Those in the crowd who heard these words were saying, "This has to be the Prophet." Others said, "He is the Messiah!" But others were saying, "The Messiah doesn't come from Galilee, does he? Don't the Scriptures tell us that the Messiah comes from David's line and from Bethlehem, David's village?" So there was a split in the crowd over him. Some went so far as wanting to arrest him, but no one laid a hand on him.

That's when the Temple police reported back to the high priests and Pharisees, who demanded, "Why didn't you bring him with you?"

The police answered, "Have you heard the way he talks? We've never heard anyone speak like this man."

The Pharisees said, "Are you carried away like the rest of the rabble? You don't see any of the leaders believing in him, do you? Or any from the Pharisees? It's only this crowd, ignorant of God's Law, that is taken in by him—and damned."

Nicodemus, the man who had come to Jesus earlier and was both a ruler and a Pharisee, spoke up. "Does our Law decide about a man's guilt without first listening to him and finding out what he is doing?"

But they cut him off. "Are you also campaigning for the Galilean? Examine the evidence. See if any prophet ever comes from Galilee."

Then they all went home.

Jesus went across to Mount Olives, but he was soon back in

the Temple again. Swarms of people came to him. He sat down and taught them.

The religion scholars and Pharisees led in a woman who had been caught in an act of adultery. They stood her in plain sight of everyone and said, "Teacher, this woman was caught red-handed in the act of adultery. Moses, in the Law, gives orders to stone such persons. What do you say?" They were trying to trap him into saying something incriminating so they could bring charges against him.

Jesus bent down and wrote with his finger in the dirt. They kept at him, badgering him. He straightened up and said, "The sinless one among you, go first: Throw the stone." Bending down again, he wrote some more in the dirt.

Hearing that, they walked away, one after another, beginning with the oldest. The woman was left alone. Jesus stood up and spoke to her. "Woman, where are they? **Does no one condemn you?**"

"No one, Master."

"Neither do I," said Jesus. "Go on your way. From now on, don't sin."

THINK   "Does no one condemn you?"

- What is your immediate response to this question?
- Why do you think you responded in this way?
- How do you feel about the characters in this passage?

    The crowd?

    The Temple police?

    The Pharisees and religion scholars?

    The woman caught red-handed?

    Jesus?

- How does knowing that "they were trying to trap him" change your perspective on the situation the Pharisees brought to Jesus?
- Besides Jesus, the other characters in the final portion of the passage are the Pharisees and the woman. Which of these do you resemble most often?

READ

From *Intimate Moments with the Savior*, by Ken Gire[1]

The ruckus can be heard a block away, interrupting the peaceful yawn of the city. And into the midst of the crowd that has gathered to hear Jesus teach, she is thrown.

Barefoot and disheveled. Sweaty from the struggle, she stands there, a mop of hair hanging in her face. Her jaw is fixed. Her teeth clenched. Her lips pressed into thin lines of resistance. Her nostrils flared in breathy defiance.

"Adulteress!" they charge. "Caught in the act!"

But caught by whom? And why?

The teachers and Pharisees appeal to the Law and call for the death penalty. But for a person to be put to death the Law requires that there be at least two eyewitnesses. Eyewitnesses to the very act of adultery.

Can you picture the scene? Peeping Pharisees nosing around her windowsill. How long did they watch? How much did they see? And were not their hearts filled with adultery when they eavesdropped on the clandestine rendezvous? At least two witnessed the act. Yet without compunction for the sin. Or compassion for the sinner.

When they had seen enough, these guardians of morality stormed the door to the bedroom where she lay naked and defenseless. She struggled as they wrestled to subdue her. They pushed her into her clothes like a pig into a gunny sack to be taken, kicking and squealing, to market.

Thus she arrives at the temple. Torn from the privacy of a stolen embrace and thrust into public shame.

This is it, she tells herself, this is the end. Her fate forever at the hands of men. From their hands she has received bread. Now it is to be stones.

And so she stands there, sullen, her eyes deep sinkholes of hate. And every eye that circles her returns the searing hate, branding a scarlet letter onto her soul. Every eye, that is, except for the eyes of Jesus. . . .

The silence is deafening; the drama, intense. With his finger he writes in the sand. The necks of the righteous crane to decipher the writing. What he writes will forever remain a mystery. Maybe it is the sins the crowd has committed. Maybe it is a quote from Moses. Maybe it is the names of the prominent leaders there. Whatever he writes is for their eyes, not ours.

Jesus stands up. All eyes are fixed on him.

At last he responds, "If any one of you is without sin, let him be the first to throw a stone at her."

One by one the stones thud to the ground. And one by one the men leave. Starting with the oldest, perhaps because they are the wisest—or the most guilty.

Jesus stoops to write again. This time it is only for her eyes.

They are alone now—lawbreaker and lawgiver. And the only one qualified to condemn her, doesn't. . . .

"Has no one condemned you?" he asks.

Timid words stumble from her lips, "No one, sir."

She waits for a reply. Certainly a sermon must be gathering momentum in the wings. But no sermon comes.

What comes are words of grace. "Neither do I condemn you," and words of truth, that her life of sin needs to be left behind. . . .

She looks into his face. His forehead relaxes. It has been an ordeal for him, too. He takes a breath and his smile seems to say, "Go, you're free now."

She opens her mouth to say something. But the words don't come. . . .

There are no tears as she leaves. Years later there will be. At odd moments during the day: when she looks at her children asleep in their beds; when she waves good-bye to her husband as he walks to work in the morning; when she kneads bread in the solitude of her kitchen.

A marriage she never would have had . . . a family she never would have had . . . a life she never would have had—were it not for such a wonderful savior. A savior who stood up for her when others wanted to stone her. A Savior who stooped to pick her up and send her on her way, forgiven.

THINK   "Does no one condemn you?"

- What does Gire's meditation on the passage add to your feelings about this woman and her accusers?
- What does it add to your feelings about the Savior?
- Have you ever been the "peeping Pharisee"? Think about a specific person, place, and time.
- Have you ever been the "woman caught in the act"? What was the resolution to that situation?

READ

From *The Safest Place on Earth*, by Larry Crabb[2]

Everything in spiritual community is reversed from the world's order. It is our weakness, not our competence, that moves others; our sorrows, not our blessings, that break down the barriers of fear and shame that keep us apart; our admitted failures, not our paraded successes, that bind us together in hope.

A spiritual community, *a church*, is full of broken people who turn their chairs toward each other because they know they cannot make it alone. These broken people journey together with their wounds and worries and washouts visible, but are able to see beyond the brokenness to something alive and good, something whole.

Each of us is wounded. For every one of us, ruthless honesty about what is happening inside of us will lead us to brokenness. In a spiritual community, people don't merely talk about woundedness and brokenness. They leave their comfort zones and expose the specifics, not to everyone, but to at least one other person.

It's terrifying to do so. It seems weak, so unnecessary, so morbid and self-criticizing. Worse, in many eyes, to admit brokenness means to admit a poor relationship with God. We often *hear* that brokenness is the pathway to a deeper relationship with God, but we rarely see it modeled. I sometimes think we want others to believe that we know God by demonstrating how unbroken we are.

But we've all been wounded. We've all failed. Rejection has brought out depths of anger we didn't know were in us. We've sobbed over unkindness and resolved to never let anyone treat us like that again. Our souls have withered under the heat of someone's disdain. Criticism has made us feel worthless, and we've either backed away from involvement or taken life on with defensive arrogance.

We protect our wounds with all the fierceness of a lioness

watching over her cubs. And because it is nearly impossible to see who we are as separate from those wounds, we think we are protecting our *selves* when in fact we are preserving our *wounds*.

THINK   "Does no one condemn you?"

- Does your experience with church sound anything like what Crabb described?
- Do you even desire your church to be like what he described? Why or why not?
- "But we've all been wounded." Spend some time with that statement. What are the wounds that come to mind for you? Do you protect them?
- Do you ever feel condemned at church or in community with others? What makes you feel that way?
- What does it mean to live out the truth that Jesus not only doesn't condemn you but also forgives you? What would it feel like to experience that kind of acceptance and freedom in church?

READ

From *Abba's Child*, by Brennan Manning[3]

The life of Jesus suggests that to be like Abba is to show compassion. Donald Gray expresses this: "Jesus reveals in an exceptionally human life what it is to live a divine life, a compassionate life."[4]

Scripture points to an intimate connection between compassion and forgiveness. According to Jesus, a distinctive sign of Abba's child is the willingness to forgive our enemies: "Love your enemies and do good . . . and you will be sons of the Most High for he himself is kind to the ungrateful and the wicked" (Luke 6:35). In the Lord's Prayer we acknowledge the primary characteristic of Abba's children when we pray, "Forgive us our trespasses as we forgive those who trespass against us." Jesus presents His Abba as the model for our forgiveness: the king in Matthew 18 who forgives a fantastic sum, an unpayable debt, the God who forgives without limit (the meaning of seventy times seven).

God calls His children to a countercultural lifestyle of forgiveness in a world that demands an eye for an eye—and worse. But if loving God is the first commandment, and loving our neighbor proves our love for God, and if it is easy to love those who love us, then loving our enemies must be the filial badge that identifies Abba's children.

The summons to live as forgiven and forgiving children is radically inclusive. It is addressed not only to the wife whose husband forgot their wedding anniversary but also to the parents whose child was slaughtered by a drunken driver, to the victims of slanderous accusations and to the poor living in filthy boxes who see the rich drive by in Mercedes, to the sexually molested and to spouses shamed by the unfaithfulness of their partner, to believers who have been terrorized with blasphemous images of an unbiblical deity and to the mother in El Salvador whose daughter's body was returned to her horribly butchered, to elderly couples who lost all their savings because their bankers were thieves and to the woman whose alcoholic husband squandered their inheritance, to those who are objects of ridicule, discrimination, and prejudice.

The demands of forgiveness are so daunting that they seem humanly impossible. The exigencies of forgiveness are simply beyond the capacity of ungraced human will. Only reckless confidence in a Source greater than ourselves can empower us to forgive the wounds inflicted by others. In boundary moments such as these there is only one place to go—Calvary.

THINK   "Does no one condemn you?"

- Maybe you've been the one "caught" and then shown incredible grace by the Lord. His last words to the adulterous woman in John 8 were "From now on, don't sin" (verse 11). Are there people you need to show grace to by releasing them from your anger and bitterness? People who've wounded you?
- How can you live this question and learn to accept others who are just as imperfect as you?
- How does a relationship change when forgiveness enters into it? How does Jesus' sacrifice—his forgiveness of sins—truly empower you to forgive others instead of condemn them? Is that always easy to do? Why or why not?

PRAY

Look back at the "Think" sections. Ruminate on your responses.
Let them distill into a prayer, and then write that prayer below.

Mighty rushing wind . . .

The issue of prayer is not prayer; the issue of prayer is God.

ABRAHAM HESCHEL

LIVE   "Does no one condemn you?"

The challenge now is to take this question further along—to live out this question. Think of one thing, *just one*, that you can personally do to wrestle with the question, inhabit the character of it, and live it in everyday life. In the following space, jot down your thoughts on this "one thing." Read the Scripture and quotes that follow for additional inspiration. During the coming week, pray about this "one thing," talk with a close friend about it, and learn to live the question.

One thing . . .

With the arrival of Jesus, the Messiah, that fateful dilemma is resolved. Those who enter into Christ's being-here-for-us no longer have to live under a continuous, low-lying black cloud. A new power is in operation. The Spirit of life in Christ, like a strong wind, has magnificently cleared the air, freeing you from a fated lifetime of brutal tyranny at the hands of sin and death.

Romans 8:1-2

Forgiveness is the fragrance the violet sheds on the heel that has crushed it.

Mark Twain

Live the questions now. Perhaps you will then gradually, without noticing it, live along some distant day into the answer.

RAINER MARIA RILKE, *LETTERS TO A YOUNG POET*

"How do you expect to see the Father?"
(John 8:19)

Before You Begin

Take some time to reflect and prepare your heart and mind for this study. Read the following Scripture passage. Soak up God's Word. There's no hurry. Then, when you're ready, turn the page and begin.

John 9:39

Jesus then said, "I came into the world to bring everything into the clear light of day, making all the distinctions clear, so that those who have never seen will see, and those who have made a great pretense of seeing will be exposed as blind."

READ

John 8:12-19

Jesus once again addressed them: "I am the world's Light. No one who follows me stumbles around in the darkness. I provide plenty of light to live in."

The Pharisees objected, "All we have is your word on this. We need more than this to go on."

Jesus replied, "You're right that you only have my word. But you can depend on it being true. I know where I've come from and where I go next. You don't know where I'm from or where I'm headed. You decide according to what you can see and touch. I don't make judgments like that. But even if I did, my judgment would be true because I wouldn't make it out of the narrowness of my experience but in the largeness of the One who sent me, the Father. That fulfills the conditions set down in God's Law: that you can count on the testimony of two witnesses. And that is what you have: You have my word and you have the word of the Father who sent me."

They said, "Where is this so-called Father of yours?"

Jesus said, "You're looking right at me and you don't see me. **How do you expect to see the Father?** If you knew me, you would at the same time know the Father."

THINK
"How do you expect to see the Father?"

- What is your immediate response to this question?
- Why do you think you responded in this way?
- Are you someone who likes things proven to you? Why do you think that is?
- In what ways are you like or unlike these Pharisees? What proof would you like to have that Jesus is who he says he is?
- What are the implications of Jesus' phrase "If you knew me . . ."? What does this say about the importance of relationship in faith?

THINK (continued)

READ

From *The Pursuit of Holiness*, by Jerry Bridges[1]

> On numerous occasions the Scriptures testify that Jesus during His
> time on earth lived a perfectly holy life. He is described as "with-
> out sin" (Hebrews 4:15); as One who "committed no sin" (1 Peter
> 2:22); and as "him who had no sin" (2 Corinthians 5:21). . . .
>
> Even more compelling, however, is Jesus' own testimony
> concerning Himself. On one occasion He looked the Pharisees
> squarely in the eye and asked, "Can any of you prove me guilty
> of sin?" (John 8:46). As someone has observed, it was not their
> failure to answer His question that is so significant, but the fact
> He dared to ask it. Here was Jesus in direct confrontation with
> the people who hated Him. He had just told them they were
> of their father the devil, and that they wanted to carry out his
> desires. Surely if any people had a reason to point out to Him
> some careless act of His or some flaw of His character, they
> would. Furthermore, Jesus asked this question in the presence
> of His disciples, who lived with Him continuously and had ample
> opportunity to observe any inconsistencies. Yet Jesus dared to
> ask the question because He knew there was only one answer.
> He was without sin.

THINK   "How do you expect to see the Father?"

- Does the evidence in this excerpt help you see the truth of who
  Jesus is? Why or why not?
- Can evidence alone help someone discover the truth about
  who Jesus is? Explain.
- Why is it critical to see Jesus for who he is before you can know
  God? What about all the people who never hear about Jesus?
  Do they miss out on the God-infused life?

THINK (continued)

READ

From *Mere Christianity*, by C. S. Lewis[2]

A man who was merely a man and said the sort of things Jesus said wouldn't be a great moral teacher. He would either be a lunatic on the level with a man who says he's a poached egg— or else he would be the devil of hell; you must take your choice. Either this was, and is, the Son of God, or else a mad man or something worse. You can shut Him up for a demon, or you can fall at His feet and call Him Lord and God. But don't come up with any patronizing nonsense about His being a great moral teacher. He hasn't left that alternative open to us. He did not intend to.

THINK "How do you expect to see the Father?"

- Do you understand why some people see Jesus as simply a "great moral teacher"? What might you say to them after reading this?
- What in the above excerpt do you agree with? What is difficult for you to accept?
- Do you think it would have been easier or more difficult for you to see Jesus as God had you lived during the time he walked this earth? Explain your thoughts.
- What do you think blinded the Pharisees from seeing Jesus as God's Son? Does that surprise you? Why or why not?

READ

John Donne[3]

> The whole life of Christ was a continual Passion; others die
> martyrs but Christ was born a martyr. He found Golgotha, where
> he was crucified, even in Bethlehem, where he was born; for
> to his tenderness then the straws were almost as sharp as the
> thorns after, and the manger as uneasy at first as the cross at
> last. His birth and death were but one continual act, and his
> Christmas Day and his Good Friday are but the evening and
> morning of the same day.

THINK   "How do you expect to see the Father?"

- What is your initial reaction upon reading this?
- How does the Passion story define Jesus' life?
- If Jesus knew his path ultimately led to the Cross, do you think
  that might have impacted the way in which he spoke to the
  Pharisees? Explain.
- How does it make you feel to know that Jesus' mission—
  from birth to death to resurrection—was to draw you into a
  relationship with God? How do you live that out in everyday
  life?

PRAY

Look back at the "Think" sections. Ruminate on your responses.
Let them distill into a prayer, and then write that prayer below.

Giver of sight, help me see . . .

The issue of prayer is not prayer; the issue of prayer is God.

ABRAHAM HESCHEL

LIVE   "How do you expect to see the Father?"

The challenge now is to take this question further along—to live out
this question. Think of one thing, *just one*, that you can personally do
to wrestle with the question, inhabit the character of it, and live it in
everyday life. In the following space, jot down your thoughts on this
"one thing." Read the Scripture and quotes that follow for additional
inspiration. During the coming week, pray about this "one thing," talk
with a close friend about it, and learn to live the question.

One thing...

Jesus is God spelling Himself out in language that man can
understand.

S. D. Gordon

"Don't you believe that I am in the Father and the Father is in
me? The words that I speak to you aren't mere words. I don't
just make them up on my own. The Father who resides in me
crafts each word into a divine act.
    "Believe me: I am in my Father and my Father is in me.
If you can't believe that, believe what you see—these works.
The person who trusts me will not only do what I'm doing
but even greater things, because I, on my way to the Father,
am giving you the same work to do that I've been doing. You
can count on it."

John 14:10-12

Live the questions now. Perhaps you will then gradually, without
noticing it, live along some distant day into the answer.

RAINER MARIA RILKE, *LETTERS TO A YOUNG POET*

"Do you believe this?"
(John 11:26)

Before You Begin

Take some time to reflect and prepare your heart and mind for this study. Read the following Scripture passage. Soak up God's Word. There's no hurry. Then, when you're ready, turn the page and begin.

LUKE 4:18-19

God's Spirit is on me;
>   he's chosen me to preach the Message of good
>   news to the poor,
Sent me to announce pardon to prisoners and
>   recovery of sight to the blind,
To set the burdened and battered free,
>   to announce, "This is God's year to act!"

READ

John 11:1-27

A man was sick, Lazarus of Bethany, the town of Mary and her sister Martha. This was the same Mary who massaged the Lord's feet with aromatic oils and then wiped them with her hair. It was her brother Lazarus who was sick. So the sisters sent word to Jesus, "Master, the one you love so very much is sick."

When Jesus got the message, he said, "This sickness in not fatal. It will become an occasion to show God's glory by glorifying God's Son."

Jesus loved Martha and her sister and Lazarus, but oddly, when he heard that Lazarus was sick, he stayed on where he was for two more days. After the two days, he said to his disciples, "Let's go back to Judea."

They said, "Rabbi, you can't do that. The Jews are out to kill you, and you're going back?"

Jesus replied, "Are there not twelve hours of daylight? Anyone who walks in daylight doesn't stumble because there's plenty of light from the sun. Walking at night, he might very well stumble because he can't see where he's going."

He said these things, and then announced, "Our friend Lazarus has fallen asleep. I'm going to wake him up."

The disciples said, "Master, if he's gone to sleep, he'll get a good rest and wake up feeling fine." Jesus was talking about death, while his disciples thought he was talking about taking a nap.

Then Jesus became explicit: "Lazarus died. And I am glad for your sakes that I wasn't there. You're about to be given new grounds for believing. Now let's go to him."

That's when Thomas, the one called the Twin, said to his companions, "Come along. We might as well die with him."

When Jesus finally got there, he found Lazarus already four days dead. Bethany was near Jerusalem, only a couple of miles away, and many of the Jews were visiting Martha and Mary, sympathizing with them over their brother. Martha heard Jesus was coming and went out to meet him. Mary remained in the house.

Martha said, "Master, if you'd been here, my brother wouldn't have died. Even now, I know that whatever you ask God he will give you."

Jesus said, "Your brother will be raised up."

Martha replied, "I know that he will be raised up in the resurrection at the end of time."

"You don't have to wait for the End. I am, right now, Resurrection and Life. The one who believes in me, even though he or she dies, will live. And everyone who lives believing in me does not ultimately die at all. **Do you believe this?**"

"Yes, Master. All along I have believed that you are the Messiah, the Son of God who comes into the world."

THINK   "Do you believe this?"

- What is your immediate response to this question?
- Why do you think you responded in this way?
- How do you feel about Jesus' lack of hurry in going to Bethany?
- Think about these two instances from the reading when people very close to Jesus missed the meaning of his words:

    The disciples said, "Master, if he's gone to sleep, he'll get a good rest and wake up feeling fine." Jesus was talking about death, while his disciples thought he was talking about taking a nap.

    Jesus said, "Your brother will be raised up." Martha replied, "I know that he will be raised up in the resurrection at the end of time."

    If even people that close to Jesus missed what he was saying, shouldn't we take our time with his words? How can we do that?

- Earlier in John (10:10), Jesus said: "I came so they can have real and eternal life, more and better life than they ever dreamed of." Take your time with Jesus' words here so you don't miss what Jesus is really asking Martha about. Read the verses leading up to the question again, and then write what you hear Jesus saying.

• How would you answer the question "Do you believe this?"

READ

From *Waking the Dead*, by John Eldredge[1]

"The glory of God is man fully alive." (Saint Irenaeus)

When I first stumbled across this quote, my initial reaction was . . . *You're kidding me. Really?* I mean, is that what you've been told? That the purpose of God—the very thing he's staked his reputation on—is your coming fully alive? Huh. Well, that's a different take on things. It made me wonder, *What are God's intentions toward me? What is it I've come to believe about that?* Yes, we've been told any number of times that God does care, and some pretty glowing promises given to us in Scripture along those lines. But on the other hand, we have the days of our lives, and they have a way of casting a rather long shadow over our hearts when it comes to God's intentions toward us in particular. . . .

I turned to the New Testament to have another look, read for myself what Jesus said he offers. "I have come that they may have life, and have it to the full" (John 10:10). Wow. That's different from saying, "I have come to forgive you. Period." Forgiveness is awesome, but Jesus says here he came to give us *life.* Hmmm. . . . The more I looked, the more this whole theme of life jumped off the pages. I mean, it's *everywhere.* . . .

I began to get the feeling of a man who's been robbed. I'm well aware that it's life I *need,* and it's life I'm looking for. But the offer has gotten "interpreted" by well-meaning people to say, "Oh, well. Yes, of course. . . . God intends life for you. But that is *eternal* life, meaning, because of the death of Jesus Christ you can go to heaven when you die." And that's true . . . in a way. But it's like saying getting married means, "Because I've given you this ring, you will be taken care of in your retirement." And in the meantime? Isn't there a whole lot more to the relationship *in the meantime?* . . .

Jesus doesn't locate his offer to us only in some distant future after we've slogged our way through our days here on earth. He talks about a life available to us *in this age.* So does

Paul: "Godliness has value for all things, holding promise for both the present life and the life to come" (I Tim. 4:8). Our *present* life and the next. When we hear the words *eternal life,* most of us tend to interpret that as "a life that waits for us in eternity." But *eternal* means "unending," not "later." The Scriptures use the term to mean we can never lose. It's a life that can't be taken from us. The offer is life, and that life starts *now.*

From *The Divine Conspiracy*, by Dallas Willard[2]

The real question, I think, is whether God would establish a bar code type of arrangement at all. It is we who are in danger: in danger of missing the fullness of life offered to us. Can we seriously believe that God *would* establish a plan for us that essentially bypasses the awesome needs of present human life and leaves human character untouched? Would he leave us even temporarily marooned with no help in our kind of world, with our kinds of problems: psychological, emotional, social, and global? Can we believe that the essence of Christian faith and salvation covers nothing but death and after? Can we believe that being saved really has nothing whatever to do with the kinds of persons we are?

THINK   "Do you believe this?"

- How do these passages make you feel?
- Have you ever heard anything like this before? If so, where and when?
- What has been your definition of eternal life, this gift Jesus came to give us?
- If eternal means "unending" and not "later," what difference does that make in your life?
- Is it easy to believe this? Why or why not?

THINK (continued)

READ

From *The Jesus I Never Knew,* by Philip Yancey[3]

The story of Lazarus has a unique "staged" quality about it. Usually when Jesus got word of a sick person he responded immediately, sometimes changing plans in order to accommodate the request. This time, after receiving word of the illness of one of his good friends, he lingered in another town for two more days. He did so intentionally, in full knowledge that the delay would result in Lazarus's death. John included Jesus' cryptic explanation to his disciples, "Lazarus is dead, and for your sake I am glad I was not there, so that you may believe." Deliberately, he let Lazarus die and his family grieve.

In another context Luke contrasts the personality types of Lazarus's two sisters: Martha, the obsessive hostess who scurries about the kitchen, and Mary the contemplative, content to sit at the feet of Jesus. In a time of tragedy, the personality types held true. Martha rushed down the road to meet Jesus' party outside the village. "Lord," she chided him, "if you had been here, my brother would not have died." Some time later Mary caught up and, poignantly, said exactly the same words: "Lord, if you had been here, my brother would not have died."

The sisters' words carry the tone of accusation, the indictment of a God who did not answer prayer. No matter how hard we try, those of us who grieve cannot avoid words like "if only." *If only he had missed that flight. If only she had quit smoking. If only I had taken time to say "Good-bye."* In this case, Mary and Martha had a clear target for their "if onlys": the Son of God himself, their friend, who could have prevented the death.

THINK   "Do you believe this?"

• What are some "if onlys" you have addressed to the Son of God himself?

• What do you think an understanding of Jesus being the Resurrection and the Life does to the "if onlys"?

• Do you find it difficult to accept that Jesus' gift of eternal life is enough? How do you deal with the challenges and tragedies that still come in life? Does "believing" ever seem insufficient for you? Explain.

READ

From *Abba's Child*, by Brennan Manning[4]

The resurrection of Jesus must be experienced as more than a past historical event. Otherwise, "it is robbed of its impact on the present."[5] In his book *True Resurrection*, Anglican theologian H. A. Williams wrote, "That is why for most of the time resurrection means little to us. It is remote and isolated. And that is why for the majority of people it means nothing. . . . People do well to be skeptical of beliefs not anchored in present experience."[6]

On the other hand, if the central saving act of Christian faith is relegated to the future with the fervent hope that Christ's resurrection is the pledge of our own and that one day we shall reign with Him in glory, then the risen One is pushed safely out of the present. Limiting the resurrection either to the past or to the future makes the present risenness of Jesus largely irrelevant, safeguards us from interference with the ordinary rounds and daily routine of our lives, and preempts communion now with Jesus as a living person.

In other words, the resurrection needs to be experienced as present risenness. If we take seriously the word of the risen Christ, "Know that I am with you always; yes, to the end of time" (Matthew 28:20), we should expect that He will be actively present in our lives. If our faith is alive and luminous, we will be alert to moments, events, and occasions when the power of resurrection is brought to bear on our lives. Self-absorbed and inattentive, we fail to notice the subtle ways in which Jesus is snagging our attention.

William Barry wrote, "We must school ourselves to pay attention to our experience of life in order to discern the touch of God or what Peter Berger calls the *rumor of angels* from all the other influences on our experience"[7] (emphasis added).

THINK   "Do you believe this?"

- "Limiting the resurrection either to the past or to the future." Which of these two options best describes you? Why?
- How does the phrase "present risenness" make you feel?
- Think about how much of your time could be described as "self-absorbed and inattentive." Are you pleased with this assessment?
- Barry says that "we must school ourselves to pay attention to our experience of life in order to discern . . . the rumor of angels." First of all, have you had moments when you did pay attention and experienced the present risenness of Christ? List a few. Second, what are some practical ways in which you can "school" yourself not to miss these?

PRAY

Look back at the "Think" sections. Ruminate on your responses. Let them distill into a prayer, and then write that prayer below.

Help my unbelief...

The issue of prayer is not prayer; the issue of prayer is God.

ABRAHAM HESCHEL

LIVE   "Do you believe this?"

The challenge now is to take this question further along—to live out this question. Think of one thing, *just one*, that you can personally do to wrestle with the question, inhabit the character of it, and live it in everyday life. In the following space, jot down your thoughts on this "one thing." Read the Scripture and quotes that follow for additional inspiration. During the coming week, pray about this "one thing," talk with a close friend about it, and learn to live the question.

One thing...

We're not keeping this quiet, not on your life. Just like the psalmist who wrote, "I believed it, so I said it," we say what we believe. And what we believe is that the One who raised up the Master Jesus will just as certainly raise us up with you, alive.

2 Corinthians 4:13-14

We are born believing. A man bears beliefs, as a tree bears apples.

Ralph Waldo Emerson

Live the questions now. Perhaps you will then gradually, without noticing it, live along some distant day into the answer.

RAINER MARIA RILKE, *LETTERS TO A YOUNG POET*

LESSON 7

"Do you understand what I have done to you?"
(John 13:12)

Before You Begin

Take some time to reflect and prepare your heart and mind for this study. Read the following Scripture passage. Soak up God's Word. There's no hurry. Then, when you're ready, turn the page and begin.

MATTHEW 25:37-40

"Then those 'sheep' are going to say, 'Master, what are you talking about? When did we ever see you hungry and feed you, thirsty and give you a drink? And when did we ever see you sick or in prison and come to you?' Then the King will say, 'I'm telling the solemn truth: Whenever you did one of these things to someone overlooked or ignored, that was me—you did it to me.'"

READ

John 13:1-17

Just before the Passover Feast, Jesus knew that the time had come to leave this world to go to the Father. Having loved his dear companions, he continued to love them right to the end. It was suppertime. The Devil by now had Judas, son of Simon the Iscariot, firmly in his grip, all set for the betrayal.

Jesus knew that the Father had put him in complete charge of everything, that he came from God and was on his way back to God. So he got up from the supper table, set aside his robe, and put on an apron. Then he poured water into a basin and began to wash the feet of the disciples, drying them with his apron. When he got to Simon Peter, Peter said, "Master, *you* wash *my* feet?"

Jesus answered, "You don't understand now what I'm doing, but it will be clear enough to you later."

Peter persisted, "You're not going to wash my feet—ever!"

Jesus said, "If I don't wash you, you can't be part of what I'm doing."

"Master!" said Peter. "Not only my feet, then. Wash my hands! Wash my head!"

Jesus said, "If you've had a bath in the morning, you only need your feet washed now and you're clean from head to toe. My concern, you understand, is holiness, not hygiene. So now you're clean. But not every one of you." (He knew who was betraying him. That's why he said, "Not every one of you.") After he had finished washing their feet, he took his robe, put it back on, and went back to his place at the table.

Then he said, "**Do you understand what I have done to you?** You address me as 'Teacher' and 'Master,' and rightly so. That is what I am. So if I, the Master and Teacher, washed your feet, you must now wash each other's feet. I've laid down a pattern for you. What I've done, you do. I'm only pointing out the obvious. A servant is not ranked above his master; an employee doesn't give orders to the employer. If you understand what I'm telling you, act like it—and live a blessed life."

THINK   "Do you understand what I have done to you?"

- What is your immediate response to this question?
- Why do you think you responded in this way?
- Can you identify with Peter's "Master, *you* wash *my* feet?" in any way?
- "My concern, you understand, is holiness, not hygiene." "So if I, the Master and Teacher, washed your feet, you must now wash each other's feet. I've laid down a pattern for you." Take some time and combine these phrases into a single thought. Jesus is striving to teach a single point to his dear companions.

READ

From "The Welcome Table," by Alice Walker[1]

She was angular and lean and the color of poor gray Georgia
earth, beaten by king cotton and the extreme weather. Her elbows
were wrinkled and thick, the skin ashen but durable, like the bark
of old pines. On her face centuries were folded into the circles
around one eye, while around the other, etched and mapped as if
for print, ages more threatened again to live. Some of them there
at the church saw the age, the dotage, the missing buttons down
the front of her mildewed black dress. Others saw cooks, chauf-
feurs, maids, mistresses, children denied or smothered in the
deferential way she held her cheek to the side, toward the ground.
Many of them saw jungle orgies in an evil place, while others were
reminded of riotous anarchists looting and raping in the streets.
Those who knew the hesitant creeping up on them of the law saw
the beginning of the end of the sanctuary of Christian worship,
saw the desecration of the Holy Church, and saw an invasion of
privacy, which they struggled to believe they still kept.

Still she had come down the road toward the big white
church alone. Just herself, an old forgetful woman, nearly blind
with age. Just her and her eyes raised dully to the glittering cross
that crowned the sheer silver steeple. . . .

The reverend of the church stopped her pleasantly as she
stepped into the vestibule. Did he say, as they thought he did,
kindly, "Auntie, you know this is not your church"? As if one could
choose the wrong one. But no one remembers, for they never
spoke of it afterward, and she brushed past him anyway, as if she
had been brushing past him all her life, except this time she was
in a hurry. . . .

The young usher, never having turned anyone out of his
church before, but not even considering this job as that (after
all, she had no right to be there, certainly), went up to her and
whispered that she should leave. Did he call her "Grandma," as
later he seemed to recall he had? . . .

It was the ladies who finally did what to them had to be done. Daring their burly indecisive husbands to throw the old colored woman out they made their point. God, mother, country, earth, church. It involved all that, and well they knew it. Leather bagged and shoed, with good calfskin gloves to keep out the cold, they looked with contempt at the bloodless gray arthritic hands of the old woman, clenched loosely, restlessly in her lap. Could their husbands expect them to sit up in church with that? No, no, the husbands were quick to answer and even quicker to do their duty.

Under the old woman's arms they placed their hard fists. . . . Under the old woman's arms they raised their fists, flexed their muscular shoulders, and out she flew through the door, back under the cold blue sky. This done, the wives folded their healthy arms across their trim middles and felt at once justified and scornful. But none of them said so, for none of them ever spoke of the incident again. Inside the church it was warmer. They sang, they prayed. The protection and promise of God's impartial love grew more not less desirable as the sermon gathered fury and lashed itself out above their penitent heads.

The old woman stood at the top of the steps looking about in bewilderment. She had been singing in her head. They had interrupted her. Promptly, she began to sing again, though this time a sad song. Suddenly, however, she looked down the long gray highway and saw something interesting and delightful coming. She started to grin, toothlessly, with short giggles of joy, jumping about and slapping her hands on her knees. And soon it became apparent why she was so happy. For coming down the highway at a firm though leisurely pace was Jesus.

THINK   "Do you understand what I have done to you?"

- What is your emotional response to this passage?
- What would you like to say to the old woman?
- What would you like to say to "the ladies"?

- Do you think these "church people" understood anything about the pattern Jesus laid down for us in John 13 (see first "Read" section of this lesson)? Why or why not?
- Do you think *your* church people are any more mature?
- Is there someone that you've seen picked up and ushered out when they should have been seated and "washed"? Recount that incident.

READ

From *Ragman and Other Cries of Faith*, by Walter Wangerin Jr.[2]

Now, this is the truth: I first knew the love of my God in the love of my father.

I used to get dreadful cases of poison ivy. Angry red dots spread my limbs, erupting in bunches like mountain ranges. On my face the pustules ran an amber fluid that scabbed in amber crust. And it went into my hair, my nostrils, the backs of my hands, and so forth. Fierce cases and most debilitating itches. I was miserable.

I was also convinced that scratching the stuff spread it; so I schooled myself in stillness. Awake I could hold a position before the TV set for hours at a time. Sleeping, however, I lost control and would wake both scratching and on fire. So I conceived a plan. I had my brother tie my hands behind my back before I went to bed with ropes, belts, the bathrobe cord, tape, anything. But nothing worked. I was Houdini in my sleep, slipping the most intricate knots of my brother and scratching hell out of my flesh, I, my own assassin!

So, my mother conceived a plan. She'd heard somewhere that Fels Naptha soap was a warrior against the itch. She had *not* heard that laundry soap is supposed to rinse the skin of ivy oils within an hour of touching it; rather, she considered it a lotion. Therefore, my mother, who didn't do things by halves, worked wonderful lather of Fels Naptha and applied it to every mass of rash on my body, and so it dried, and so it caked, and so her son was mummified. It's hard to sweat under a cast of Fels Naptha. Worse, the stuff was stiff against my skin, so every move I made irritated a thousand dots, which all set up a jubilation of itching and drove me to a pitiful distraction.

More than ever, I schooled myself in stillness. I lay on my bed all the day long and thought that this was the way I would end my life.

On a particular afternoon, when I'd brought my flesh to quietness, was lying perfectly still abed, my father came into the room and sat beside me to talk with me—matters of the world, and so forth, before the dinner I would not share with the family, and so forth.

It was a nice talk. He is a kind man. I didn't move or look at him. But I could hear his voice.

Now, there are certain places on a boy's body which, try as he might, he can't keep still. On that place on my body, there was, at that time, one poison ivy dot. And that bodily part began to move. So that single poison ivy dot began to itch.

This was more than I could take. In a moment, all the plans of the world and all the remedies failed. Life was very bleak. Without turning my head, without so much as a sob or a groan, I began to cry. The tears trailed down my temple and pooled in my ear. I thought I would die soon.

But then I heard a strangled sound to my left.

It was my father. He'd risen to his feet. His hands were up and empty. His face was so full of anguish, seeing my tears, that my own heart went out to the man. He turned, turned fully round in the bedroom, seeming so hopeless; and then he bolted for the door, crying "Calamine lotion!—hit the wood and left.

Calamine lotion. I was experienced in the ways of poison ivy. I knew that calamine lotion was utterly useless even if it could get to the rash. . . .

Nevertheless, when my father appeared again with a giant bottle of the stuff; when my father knelt down beside the bed, uncovered me, and began so gently with his own hand to rub it on; when my father's eyes damped with the tears of suffering, so that I saw with wonder that my pain had actually become his own pain and that it was our pain that had sent him rocketing to the drug store; when I saw and felt that miracle, a second miracle took place: the ivy did not itch.

Calamine lotion did not do this thing!

My father's love did this thing—and I knew it! Oh, my heart ached to have such a father, who could enter into me and hurt so much that he took my hurt away.

THINK   "Do you understand what I have done to you?"

- Have you ever had an experience like this, where someone washed you (literally or figuratively) and you were blessed in an amazing way? Recount it here in as much detail as you can.
- What kind of an imprint did it leave on your life?
- Have you ever tried to pass that grace on by "washing" someone else? Is that a rare occurrence or a frequent practice?
- If it's rare, why? What keeps you from "washing the feet" of others?

READ

From *To Be of Use*, by Marge Piercy[3]

THINK   "Do you understand what I have done to you?"

- First of all, how did the poem make you feel? Did it evoke any specific memories or thoughts?
- Imagine Jesus sitting with the twelve after washing their feet and saying words just like those in this poem. Couple those thoughts with these words of Jesus: "Learn the unforced rhythms of grace. I won't lay anything heavy or ill-fitting on you. Keep company with me and you'll learn to live freely and lightly" (Matthew 11:29-30). Are the two ideas consistent with one another? Explain your answer.
- How might learning the "unforced rhythms of grace" help you to become servant-minded? What does this look like in the everyday rhythms of life?
- Can you live with a servant heart, act on that heart, and still live "freely and lightly"? Why or why not?

PRAY

Look back at the "Think" sections. Ruminate on your responses. Let them distill into a prayer, and then write that prayer below.

Wash me, Lord . . .

The issue of prayer is not prayer; the issue of prayer is God.

ABRAHAM HESCHEL

LIVING THE QUESTIONS SERIES

LIVE   "Do you understand what I have done to you?"

The challenge now is to take this question further along—to live out this question. Think of one thing, *just one*, that you can personally do to wrestle with the question, inhabit the character of it, and live it in everyday life. In the following space, jot down your thoughts on this "one thing." Read the Scripture and quotes that follow for additional inspiration. During the coming week, pray about this "one thing," talk with a close friend about it, and learn to live the question.

One thing . . .

The great fault, I think, in our missions is that no one likes to be second.

Robert Morrison

It was fitting that I bring up the rear. I don't deserve to be included in that inner circle, as you well know, having spent all those early years trying my best to stamp God's church right out of existence.

1 Corinthians 15:9

Live the questions now. Perhaps you will then gradually, without noticing it, live along some distant day into the answer.

RAINER MARIA RILKE, *LETTERS TO A YOUNG POET*

"Are you saying this on your own, or did others tell you this about me?" (John 18:34)

Before You Begin

Take some time to reflect and prepare your heart and mind for this study. Read the following Scripture passage. Soak up God's Word. There's no hurry. Then, when you're ready, turn the page and begin.

Joshua 24:14-15

"So now: Fear GOD. Worship him in total commitment. Get rid of the gods your ancestors worshiped on the far side of The River (the Euphrates) and in Egypt. You, worship GOD.

"If you decide that it's a bad thing to worship GOD, then choose a god you'd rather serve—and do it today. . . . As for me and my family, we'll worship GOD."

READ

John 18:28-40

They led Jesus then from Caiaphas to the Roman governor's palace. It was early morning. They themselves didn't enter the palace because they didn't want to be disqualified from eating the Passover. So Pilate came out to them and spoke. "What charge do you bring against this man?"

They said, "If he hadn't been doing something evil, do you think we'd be here bothering you?"

Pilate said, "You take him. Judge him by *your* law."

The Jews said, "We're not allowed to kill anyone." (This would confirm Jesus' word indicating the way he would die.)

Pilate went back into the palace and called for Jesus. He said, "Are you the 'King of the Jews'?"

Jesus answered, **"Are you saying this on your own, or did others tell you this about me?"**

Pilate said, "Do I look like a Jew? Your people and your high priests turned you over to me. What did you do?"

"My kingdom," said Jesus, "doesn't consist of what you see around you. If it did, my followers would fight so that I wouldn't be handed over to the Jews. But I'm not that kind of king, not the world's kind of king."

Then Pilate said, "So, are you a king or not?"

Jesus answered, "You tell me. Because I am King, I was born and entered the world so that I could witness to the truth. Everyone who cares for truth, who has any feeling for the truth, recognizes my voice."

Pilate said, "What is truth?"

Then he went back out to the Jews and told them, "I find nothing wrong in this man. It's your custom that I pardon one prisoner at Passover. Do you want me to pardon the 'King of the Jews'?"

They shouted back, "Not this one, but Barabbas!" Barabbas was a Jewish freedom fighter.

THINK   "Are you saying this on your own, or did others tell you this about me?"

- What is your immediate response to this question?
- Why do you think you responded in this way?
- Pilate was led into this drama by forces beyond his knowledge. What is your impression of Pilate based on his questions and responses?
- What is your impression of Jesus based on his?
- Think about this scene. You've got the Jews on one side and Jesus on the other. And who does that leave in the middle? Have you ever been that person in the middle? What was that like?

READ

From *When the Heart Waits*, by Sue Monk Kidd[1]

As I sat on the bench that day beneath the low-slung gray sky, everything was fomenting, turning end over like the paper cup I had watched in the street. And suddenly, at the height of my chaos, I began to entertain the overwhelming question confronting me. I had been circling it for a long time, but now, at last, I walked right into the center of it. It was a dangerous thing to do, for those who enter the heart of a sacred question and feel the searing heat it gives off are usually compelled to live on into the answer.

Is it possible, I asked myself, *that I'm being summoned from some deep and holy place within? Am I being asked to enter a new passage in the spiritual life—the journey from false self to true self? Am I being asked to dismantle old masks and patterns and unfold a deeper, more authentic self—the one God created me to be? Am I being compelled to disturb my inner universe in quest of the undiscovered being who clamors from within?*

Unfortunately, there has been little emphasis on this summons within Christian circles. When it comes, we don't understand that we're being thrust into personal transformation, into the task of birthing an "I" that is not yet. We write it off as just another predicament or plight—perhaps the result of burnout or our dissatisfaction with life.

I believe, however, that in such a summons we're actually being presented with a spiritual development task. We're being asked to unfold a deeper self—what we might call the life of Christ within us.

To embark on this task involves a deep and profound movement of soul that takes us from an identification with the collective "they" to a discovery of the individual "I," and finally, as we shall eventually see, to an embracing of the compassionate "we." This task is truly one of the more precarious and mysterious pathways in the spiritual life, for how it's navigated radically affects one's alignment with oneself, with God, and with the world.

THINK   "Are you saying this on your own, or did others tell you this about me?"

- Have you had a moment like Sue Monk Kidd's when something or someone summoned you to be more than you've been? Explain.
- Did the moment feel "precarious" and "mysterious" to you?
- How did you respond to the moment? Did you even begin to "navigate" it?

READ

From *The Ragamuffin Gospel*, by Brennan Manning[2]

The second journey begins when we know we cannot live the afternoon of life according to the morning program. We are aware that we have only a limited amount of time left to accomplish that which is really important—and that awareness illumines for us what really matters, what really counts. . . .

For the Christian, this second journey usually occurs between the ages of thirty and sixty and is often accompanied by a second call from the Lord Jesus. The second call invites us to a serious reflection on the nature and quality of our faith in the gospel of grace, our hope in the new and not yet, and our love for God and people. The second call is a summons to a deeper, more mature commitment of faith where the naiveté, first fervor, and untested idealism of the morning and the first commitment have been seasoned with pain, rejection, failure, loneliness, and self-knowledge.

THINK   *"Are you saying this on your own, or did others tell you this about me?"*

- Do you agree with Manning's "between the ages of thirty and sixty" framework? Why or why not?
- The word "summons" keeps surfacing in these readings. Think about your moment again (see previous "Think" section). Who or what was it that summoned you?
- If you're in the midst of what Manning calls "the second call," what questions are you asking? What truths are you struggling with? What are you saying now "on your own" that before only "others" told you about?
- Has there been a pressure on the part of others to bring you back in line?

THINK (continued)

READ

From *Reliving the Passion*, by Walter Wangerin Jr.[3]

Behold the people! Though they think themselves the force of the morning, in charge of things (by virtue of their numbers and their noise), they are in fact being put to a test which shall reveal the truth beneath their words, the reality beneath their self-assumptions and all their pretense.

Behold the nature of the breed!

A crowd has gathered at the Praetorium, a rabble, an obstreperous delegation of Judeans whose presence complicates Pilate's inclination to release Jesus. These crowds are volatile. Instead of a simple release, then, a choice is offered the people. Let the people feel in charge; let the people decide. The Governor will, according to a traditional Passover amnesty, free one prisoner. Which will it be—

Jesus of Nazareth?—whom they have falsely accused of treason against the Empire?

Or Barabbas?—treasonous in fact, one who committed murder for the cause?

If they choose the latter, their loyalties to the Empire (which Jesus is supposed to have offended) are revealed a vile sham, and these are no more than temporizing hypocrites, pretending any virtue to satisfy a private end.

But the Governor will release only one prisoner. Which will it be?

Jesus—who is the Son of the Father, who is the Kingdom of God come near unto them?

Or Barabbas—whose name means "the son of a (human) father," flesh itself, the fleshly pretensions to god—like, personal power in the kingdoms of the world?

This, precisely, is the timeless choice of humankind.

If they choose the latter, they choose humanity over divinity. They choose one who will harm them over one who would heal them.

If they choose Barabbas, they choose the popular revolutionary hero, the swashbuckler, the pirate, merry Robin Hood, the blood-lusty rake, the law-flout, violence glorified, appetites satisfied, James Bond, Billy Jack, Clint Eastwood, Rambo, the celebrated predator, the one who "turns them on," over one who asks them to "deny themselves and die." They choose (voluntarily!) entertainment over worship, self-satisfaction over sacrificial love, getting things over giving things, being served over serving, "feeling good about myself" and having it all and gaining the whole world and rubbing elbows with the rich rather than rubbing the wounds of the poor.

The choice is before them. And they think the choice is external, this man or that man. In fact, the choice is terribly internal: this nature or that one, good folks or people essentially selfish and evil, therefore. It's an accurate test of their character. How they choose is who they are.

THINK   "Are you saying this on your own, or did others tell you this about me?"

- Think about people you know in the "morning" of their life. Does that describe "how they choose"?
- Think of some examples of that type of seeking or behavior on your part. Write down a few of the memorable ones. You might even view this as an act of confession.
- What does the phrase "How they choose is who they are" mean to you?
- Describe what it means to own your faith. What roles do your upbringing and the people around you play in this? What influences make it difficult to choose your response to the faith questions?

THINK (continued)

READ

From *Journey of the Magi*, by T. S. Eliot[4]

A cold coming we had of it,
Just the worst time of the year
For a journey, and such a long journey:
The ways deep and the weather sharp,
The very dead of winter.
And the camels galled, sore-footed, refractory,
Lying down in the melting snow.
There were times we regretted
The summer palaces on slopes, the terraces,
And the silken girls bringing sherbert.
Then the camel men cursing and grumbling
And running away, and wanting their liquor and women,
And the night-fires going out, and the lack of shelters,
And the cities hostile and the towns unfriendly
And the villages dirty and charging high prices:
A hard time we had of it.
At the end we preferred to travel all night,
Sleeping in snatches,
With the voices singing in our ears, saying
That this was all folly.

Then at dawn we came down to a temperate valley,
Wet, below the snow line, smelling of vegetation;
With a running stream and a water-mill beating the darkness,
And three trees on the low sky,
And an old white horse galloped away in the meadow.
Then we came to a tavern with vine-leaves over the lintel,
Six hands at an open door dicing for pieces of silver,
And feet kicking the empty wine-skins.
But there was no information, and so we continued
And arrived at evening, not a moment too soon
Finding the place; it was (you may say) satisfactory.

All this was a long time ago, I remember,
And I would do it again, but set down
This set down
This: were we led all that way for
Birth or Death? There was a Birth, certainly,
We had evidence and no doubt. I had seen birth and death,
But had thought they were different; this Birth was
Hard and bitter agony for us, like Death, our death.
We returned to our places, these Kingdoms,
But no longer at ease here, in the old dispensation,
With an alien people clutching their gods.
I should be glad of another death.

THINK   "Are you saying this on your own, or did others tell
           you this about me?"

- Eliot describes the journeying in terms of a death and con-
  cludes with "I should be glad of another death." What is your
  reaction to these words?
- What voices have you heard along the way that have tried to
  convince or persuade you of the "folly" of your journey? What
  have they said? How have you responded?

PRAY

Look back at the "Think" sections. Ruminate on your responses.
Let them distill into a prayer, and then write that prayer below.

Lord, I want to know you . . .

The issue of prayer is not prayer; the issue of prayer is God.

Abraham Heschel

LIVE

"Are you saying this on your own, or did others tell you this about me?"

The challenge now is to take this question further along—to live out this question. Think of one thing, *just one*, that you can personally do to wrestle with the question, inhabit the character of it, and live it in everyday life. In the following space, jot down your thoughts on this "one thing." Read the Scripture and quotes that follow for additional inspiration. During the coming week, pray about this "one thing," talk with a close friend about it, and learn to live the question.

One thing . . .

Faith is to believe what you do not see; the reward of faith is to see what you believe.

St. Augustine

Barricade the road that goes Nowhere;
  grace me with your clear revelation.
I choose the true road to Somewhere,
  I post your road signs at every curve and corner.
I grasp and cling to whatever you tell me;
  GOD, don't let me down!

Psalm 119:29-31

Live the questions now. Perhaps you will then gradually, without noticing it, live along some distant day into the answer.

RAINER MARIA RILKE, *LETTERS TO A YOUNG POET*

"Woman, why do you weep?"
(John 20:15)

Before You Begin

Take some time to reflect and prepare your heart and mind for this study. Read the following Scripture passage. Soak up God's Word. There's no hurry. Then, when you're ready, turn the page and begin.

2 CORINTHIANS 2:17

We stand in Christ's presence when we speak; God looks us in the face. We get what we say straight from God and say it as honestly as we can.

READ

John 20:1-18

Early in the morning on the first day of the week, while it was still dark, Mary Magdalene came to the tomb and saw that the stone was moved away from the entrance. She ran at once to Simon Peter and the other disciple, the one Jesus loved, breathlessly panting, "They took the Master from the tomb. We don't know where they've put him."

Peter and the other disciple left immediately for the tomb. They ran, neck and neck. The other disciple got to the tomb first, outrunning Peter. Stooping to look in, he saw the pieces of linen cloth lying there, but he didn't go in. Simon Peter arrived after him, entered the tomb, observed the linen cloths lying there, and the kerchief used to cover his head not lying with the linen cloths but separate, neatly folded by itself. Then the other disciple, the one who had gotten there first, went into the tomb, took one look at the evidence, and believed. No one yet knew from the Scripture that he had to rise from the dead. The disciples then went back home.

But Mary stood outside the tomb weeping. As she wept, she knelt to look into the tomb and saw two angels sitting there, dressed in white, one at the head, the other at the foot of where Jesus' body had been laid. They said to her, "Woman, why do you weep?"

"They took my Master," she said, "and I don't know where they put him." After she said this, she turned away and saw Jesus standing there. But she didn't recognize him.

Jesus spoke to her, "**Woman, why do you weep?** Who are you looking for?"

She, thinking that he was the gardener, said, "Mister, if you took him, tell me where you put him so I can care for him."

Jesus said, "Mary."

Turning to face him, she said in Hebrew, "*Rabboni!*" meaning "Teacher!"

Jesus said, "Don't cling to me, for I have not yet ascended to the Father. Go to my brothers and tell them, 'I ascend to my Father and your Father, my God and your God.'"

Mary Magdalene went, telling the news to the disciples: "I saw the Master!" And she told them everything he said to her.

THINK   "Woman, why do you weep?"

- What is your immediate response to this question?
- Why do you think you responded in this way?
- When was the last time you "ran after" something or someone? Describe it in detail.
- When was the last time you "wept" for something or someone? Describe it in detail.
- Jesus asked Mary, "Why do you weep?" What do you make of a question like that? Notice that it's the very same question that the angels asked her.

READ

From *Telling Secrets*, by Frederick Buechner[1]

One November morning in 1936 when I was ten years old, my father got up early, put on a pair of gray slacks and a maroon sweater, opened the door to look in briefly on my younger brother and me, who were playing a game in our room, and then went down into the garage where he turned on the engine of the family Chevy and sat down on the running board to wait for the exhaust to kill him. Except for a memorial service for his Princeton class the next spring, by which time we had moved away to another part of the world altogether, there was no funeral because on both my mother's side and my father's there was no church connection of any kind and funerals were simply not part of the tradition. He was cremated, his ashes buried in a cemetery in Brooklyn, and I have no idea who if anybody was present. I know only that my mother, brother, and I were not.

There was no funeral to mark his death and put a period at the end of the sentence that had been his life, and as far as I can remember, once he had died my mother, brother, and I rarely talked about him much ever again, either to each other or to anybody else. It made my mother too sad to talk about him, and since there was already more than enough sadness to go round, my brother and I avoided the subject with her as she avoided it for her own reasons also with us. Once in a while she would bring it up but only in very oblique ways. I remember her saying things like "You're going to have to be big boys now," and "Now things are going to be different for all of us," and to me, "You're the man of the family now," with that one little three-letter adverb freighted with more grief and anger and guilt and God knows what all else than it could possibly bear.

We didn't talk about my father with each other, and we didn't talk about him outside the family either partly at least because suicide was looked on as something a little shabby and shameful in those days. Nice people weren't supposed to get mixed up with it. My father had tried to keep it a secret himself by leaving his note to my mother in a place where only she would be likely to find it and by saying a number of times the last few weeks of his life that there was something wrong with the Chevy's exhaust system, which he was going to see if he could fix. He did this partly in hopes that his life insurance wouldn't be invalidated, which of course it was, and partly too, I guess, in hopes that his friends wouldn't find out how he had died, which of course they did. His suicide was a secret we nonetheless tried to keep as best we could, and after a while my father himself became such a secret. There were times when he almost seemed a secret we were trying to keep from each other. I suppose there were occasions when one of us said, "Remember the time he did this," or, "Remember the time he said that," but if so, I've long since forgotten them. And because words are so much a part of what we keep the past alive by, if only words to ourselves, by not speaking of what we remembered about him we soon simply stopped remembering at all, or at least *I* did.

THINK "Woman, why do you weep?"

- Write down some words that would describe your emotional response to this passage.
- Every family has secrets. Take some time here to think about a secret that you were told *not* to talk about. This may have been an overt directive or it may have been something you just felt. Try to describe it. Don't hurry here. What was the reasoning behind the "no talk" rule?
- Have you ever wept over this secret?
- How is the pain associated with this kind of situation different from the pain Mary was feeling over the loss of Jesus? How is it similar?
- Does it take strength or weakness to allow yourself to feel the pain of loss? Explain.

THINK (continued)

READ

From *The Heart Aroused*, by David Whyte[2]

Courageous speech has always held us in awe. From the first time we spoke back to our parents as angry, stuttering teens, or had to stand tongue-tied before a roomful of people, feeling naked as the day we were born. There is, after all, something bare and revealing about speech. Perhaps because we intuit the physical intimacy behind the sound of words and the way they are spoken, and that much against our wishes our words tell the listener a good deal more than we would have them know about us.

The voice emerges literally from the body as a representation of our inner world. It carries our experience from the past, our hopes and fears for the future, and the emotional resonance of the moment. If it carries none of these, it must be a masked voice, and having muted the voice, anyone listening knows intuitively we are not all there. Whether or not we try to tell the truth, the very *act* of speech is courageous because no matter what we say, we are revealed. . . .

The voice, like the eyes and the face, is traditionally a window to the soul. If, as Gerald de Nerval said, the seat of the soul is not inside a person, or outside a person, but the very place where they overlap and meet with their world, then the voice is as good a candidate as any for getting the measure of our soul life. The voice carries the emotional body of the person speaking. Without verbal explanation, but simply through sound, it tells us who is speaking, and, in the meeting room, who has come to work. The voice is as important to our identity as anything we possess. We ask ourselves if we really have a *voice* in this organization, want reassurance that we can *give voice* to our opinions, and if we cannot, speak *soto voce* to those few in whom we choose to confide.

THINK   "Woman, why do you weep?"

- How do you feel about what Whyte is saying?
- Think about two times when it was difficult to let your voice be heard—one where you did speak up and the other where you stayed silent or quiet. Describe those times.
- Think about what Whyte has said, and then think back through the passage from John 20 (see first "Read" section in this lesson). What are some resulting thoughts when the two are combined?

READ

From *The Hero Within*, by Carol Pearson[3]

To deny the pain was to hold on to it. Only by going through it, allowing it, feeling it, *speaking aloud about it*, could she learn from it and go on to feel joy and power in a new way. The hero who can do this is rewarded with much more life than the stoic macho hero who rides off into the sunset, or more classically, retreats into the "power over" position of king and never knows the intensity of real human vulnerability and love (italics added).

From *Walking on Water*, by Madeleine L'Engle[4]

My son-in-law, Alan Jones, told me a story of a Hassidic rabbi, renowned for his piety. He was unexpectedly confronted one day by one of his devoted youthful disciples. In a burst of feeling, the young disciple exclaimed, "My master, I love you!" The ancient teacher looked up from his books and asked his fervent disciple, "Do you know what hurts me, my son?"

The young man was puzzled. Composing himself, he stuttered, "I don't understand your question, Rabbi. I am trying to tell you how much you mean to me, and you confuse me with irrelevant questions."

"My question is neither confusing nor irrelevant," rejoined the rabbi, "for if you do not know what hurts me, how can you truly love me?"

From *The Awakened Heart*, by Gerald May[5]

Intending literally means stretching; it is a stretch of the will, reaching out for and opening up to that which we desire. We are likely to think of intention as "going for it," trying to make something happen. That is willful intention; the stretching is grasping, manipulative, forceful. Because love comes as a gift, intention toward love is different. It involves yielding as well as stretching; it is reaching out with open hands, stretching oneself open in willingness.

Intention needs space within which to express itself. It also requires two other things: human awakening and divine grace. Awakening is needed for appreciation; we cannot be intentional when we are asleep. Grace is needed for empowerment: for making intention possible in the first place, and for bringing it to fruition. With space, awakening, and grace, intention becomes our *haqqodesh*, our holy ground.

THINK   "Woman, why do you weep?"

- These three readings all touch on a similar theme. What do you hear in them?
- Can you hear Jesus asking you the question he asked Mary?
- The space is provided here; God's grace is always present. Are you awake enough to "say aloud" why you weep inside? Spending some time here might just lead you to "*haqqodesh*, . . . holy ground."

PRAY

Look back at the "Think" sections. Ruminate on your responses.
Let them distill into a prayer, and then write that prayer below.

Master, well acquainted with grief . . .

The issue of prayer is not prayer; the issue of prayer is God.

ABRAHAM HESCHEL

LIVE   "Woman, why do you weep?"

The challenge now is to take this question further along—to live out this question. Think of one thing, *just one*, that you can personally do to wrestle with the question, inhabit the character of it, and live it in everyday life. In the following space, jot down your thoughts on this "one thing." Read the Scripture and quotes that follow for additional inspiration. During the coming week, pray about this "one thing," talk with a close friend about it, and learn to live the question.

One thing...

Long enough, GOD—
    you've ignored me long enough.
I've looked at the back of your head
    long enough. Long enough
I've carried this ton of trouble,
    lived with a stomach full of pain.
Long enough my arrogant enemies
    have looked down their noses at me.

Take a good look at me, GOD, my God;
    I want to look life in the eye,
So no enemy can get the best of me
    or laugh when I fall on my face.

I've thrown myself headlong into your arms—
    I'm celebrating your rescue.
I'm singing at the top of my lungs,
    I'm so full of answered prayers.

Psalm 13:1-6

The tears . . . streamed down, and I let them flow as freely as they would, making of them a pillow for my heart. On them it rested.

St. Augustine, in *Confessions*

Live the questions now. Perhaps you will then gradually, without noticing it, live along some distant day into the answer.

RAINER MARIA RILKE, *LETTERS TO A YOUNG POET*

"Do you love me?"
(John 21:17)

Before You Begin

Take some time to reflect and prepare your heart and mind for this study. Read the following Scripture passage. Soak up God's Word. There's no hurry. Then, when you're ready, turn the page and begin.

1 John 3:18-20

My dear children, let's not just talk about love; let's practice real love. This is the only way we'll know we're living truly, living in God's reality. It's also the way to shut down debilitating self-criticism, even when there is something to it. For God is greater than our worried hearts and knows more about us than we do ourselves.

READ

John 21:1-19

After this, Jesus appeared again to the disciples, this time at the Tiberias Sea (the Sea of Galilee). This is how he did it: Simon Peter, Thomas (nicknamed "Twin"), Nathanael from Cana in Galilee, the brothers Zebedee, and two other disciples were together. Simon Peter announced, "I'm going fishing."

The rest of them replied, "We're going with you." They went out and got in the boat. They caught nothing that night. When the sun came up, Jesus was standing on the beach, but they didn't recognize him.

Jesus spoke to them: "Good morning! Did you catch anything for breakfast?"

They answered, "No."

He said, "Throw the net off the right side of the boat and see what happens."

They did what he said. All of a sudden there were so many fish in it, they weren't strong enough to pull it in.

Then the disciple Jesus loved said to Peter, "It's the Master!"

When Simon Peter realized that it was the Master, he threw on some clothes, for he was stripped for work, and dove into the sea. The other disciples came in by boat for they weren't far from land, a hundred yards or so, pulling along the net full of fish. When they got out of the boat, they saw a fire laid, with fish and bread cooking on it.

Jesus said, "Bring some of the fish you've just caught." Simon Peter joined them and pulled the net to shore—153 big fish! And even will all those fish, the net didn't rip.

Jesus said, "Breakfast is ready." Not one of the disciples dared ask, "Who are you?" They knew it was the Master.

Jesus then took the bread and gave it to them. He did the same with the fish. This was now the third time Jesus had shown himself alive to the disciples since being raised from the dead.

After breakfast, Jesus said to Simon Peter, "Simon, son of

John, do you love me more than these?"

"Yes, Master, you know I love you."

Jesus said, "Feed my lambs."

He then asked a second time, "Simon, son of John, do you love me?"

"Yes, Master, you know I love you."

Jesus said, "Shepherd my sheep."

Then he said it a third time: "Simon, son of John, do you love me?"

Peter was upset that he asked for the third time, "**Do you love me?**" so he answered, "Master, you know everything there is to know. You've got to know that I love you."

Jesus said, "Feed my sheep. I'm telling you the very truth now: When you were young you dressed yourself and went wherever you wished, but when you get old you'll have to stretch out your hands while someone else dresses you and takes you where you don't want to go." He said this to hint at the kind of death by which Peter would glorify God. And then he commanded, "Follow me."

THINK   "Do you love me?"

- What is your immediate response to this question?
- Why do you think you responded in this way?
- What do you think about Peter's responses to Jesus' questions?
- Why do you think Jesus kept asking Peter this question? How might you have responded to Jesus' questions?

READ

From *Intimate Moments with the Savior*, by Ken Gire[1]

Wet and shivering, Peter reaches the shore. His eyes look down to the warm charcoal fire. A similar fire had warmed him the night of his denial. His approach is suddenly tentative and uncertain. He agonizes over that night as he presses his palms toward the heat. He yearns to talk, but the chatter of his teeth cuts his words short.

Smoke curls above the fire, entwining his thoughts into a tangle as the disciples land on the shore and join them for breakfast. They, too, are timid and quietly eat and listen. After the meal, Jesus takes Peter aside. What he says is remarkable. What he doesn't say is even more so.

He doesn't say: "Some friend you turned out to be . . . I'm really disappointed in you . . . You let me down . . . You're all talk . . . Coward . . . Boy, was I ever wrong about you . . . And you call yourself a disciple?"

Instead, he asks simply, "Do you love me?" He asks three times, once for each denial. Not to rub it in, but to give Peter an opportunity to openly confess his love. By the third time Jesus asks him, Peter gets the connection, and a flame leaps to burn him from that smoldering memory.

But Jesus is not there to inflict pain; he is there to relieve it. Jesus had seen his bitter tears when the rooster crowed. That was all he needed to see. That was repentance enough. Peter looks up, longing for the faintest glimmer of forgiveness. And in a language beyond words, in a language of love, it glows from the Savior's eyes.

"Feed my sheep, Peter." Jesus' way of saying, "I still believe in you. . . . I still think you're the right man for the job."

And with the words "Follow me," the restoration is complete. The painful memory is healed. Three and a half years ago Jesus asked Peter to follow him. The offer still stands, despite Peter's failure.

THINK   "Do you love me?"

- What do you think of Gire's meditation on this passage?
- Have you ever had someone "deny" you in a moment of great need—something along the lines of what Peter did to Jesus? (See Luke 22:54-62.) What were the particulars of that incident?
- How is that relationship right now? Has there been any restoration? Do you desire any restoration?
- What are you looking for in terms of repentance from that person? Think about Gire's words: "Jesus had seen [Peter's] bitter tears when the rooster crowed. That was all he needed to see. That was repentance enough."

READ

From "Stranger on the Shore," by Michael Card[2]

In the early morning mist they saw a stranger on the seashore.
He somehow seemed familiar asking what the night had brought.
With taut anticipation then they listened to His order
And pulling in the net found more than they had ever caught.

The one he loved first recognized the stranger there was Jesus.
He alone remembered this had happened once before.
The one who had denied Him, who had once walked on the water,
Jumped in and swam to Him, to be confronted on the shore.

You need to be confronted by the stranger on the shore.
You need to have Him search your soul, you need to hear the call.
You need to learn exactly what it means for you to follow.
You need to realize that He's asking for it all.

Then came the painful question that would pierce the soul of Simon,
A threefold chance to reaffirm the love he had denied.
The gentle eyes which saw his heart and waited for an answer,
Had seen the look upon his face the moment he had lied.

Now realize that you must face and answer all His questions,
As you stand before the stranger on the shore inside your heart.
Is a threefold chance enough to do away with your betrayals?
Or should you ask the stranger if He'll give you a new start?

You need to be confronted by the stranger on the shore.
You need to have Him search your soul, you need to hear the call.
You need to learn exactly what it means for you to follow.
You need to realize that He's asking for it all.

THINK   "Do you love me?"

- Have you ever considered yourself a denier of Christ? Think about a time in particular when, in word or deed, you denied even knowing him.
- Spend time reflecting on the chorus for a moment. Try and see the stranger on the shore confronting you, not to inflict pain but to relieve it. He's asking you to follow him. How does this make you feel?
- What do you need to hear from Jesus? A "threefold chance"? Or do you need to ask him for a "new start"?

READ

From *The Four Loves*, by C. S. Lewis[3]

In words which can still bring tears to the eyes, St. Augustine describes the desolation into which the death of his friend Nebridius plunged him (Confessions IV, 10). Then he draws a moral. This is what comes, he says, of giving one's heart to anything but God. All human beings pass away. Do not let your happiness depend on something you may lose. If love is to be a blessing, not a misery, it must be for the only Beloved who will never pass away.

Of course this is excellent sense. Don't put your goods in a leaky vessel. Don't spend too much on a house you may be turned out of. And there is no man alive who responds more naturally than I to such canny maxims. I am a safety-first creature. Of all arguments against love none makes so strong an appeal to my nature as "Careful! This might lead you to suffering."

To my nature, my temperament, yes. Not to my conscience. When I respond to that appeal I seem to myself to be a thousand miles away from Christ. If I am sure of anything I am sure that His teaching was never meant to confirm my congenital preference for safe investments and limited liabilities. I doubt whether there is anything in me that pleases Him less. And who could conceivably begin to love God on such a prudential ground—because the security (so to speak) is better? Who could even include it among the grounds for loving? Would you choose a wife or a Friend—if it comes to that, would you choose a dog—in this spirit? One must be outside the world of love, of all loves, before one thus calculates. Eros, lawless Eros, preferring the Beloved to happiness, is more like Love himself than this.

I think that this passage in the Confessions is less a part of St. Augustine's Christendom than a hangover from the high-minded Pagan philosophies in which he grew up. It is closer to Stoic "apathy" or neo-Platonic mysticism than to charity. We follow One who wept over Jerusalem and at the grave of Lazarus, and, loving all, yet had one disciple whom, in a special sense, he "loved." St. Paul has a higher authority with us than St. Augustine—St. Paul who shows no sign that he would not have suffered like a man, and no feeling that he ought not so to have suffered, if Epaphroditus had died (Phil. II, 27).

Even if it were granted that insurances against heartbreak were our highest wisdom, does God Himself offer them? Apparently not. Christ comes at last to say, "Why hast thou forsaken me?"

There is no escape along the lines St. Augustine suggests. Nor along any other lines. There is no safe investment. To love at all is to be vulnerable. Love anything, and your heart will certainly be wrung and possibly be broken. If you want to make sure of keeping it intact, you must give your heart to no one, not even to an animal. Wrap it carefully round with hobbies and little luxuries; avoid all entanglements; lock it up safe in the casket or coffin of your selfishness. But in that casket—safe, dark, motionless, airless—it will change. It will not be broken; it will become unbreakable, impenetrable, irredeemable. The alternative to tragedy, or at least to the risk of tragedy, is damnation. The only place outside Heaven where you can be perfectly safe from all the dangers and perturbations of love is Hell.

THINK   "Do you love me?"

• What is your response to Lewis's thoughts on love?
• Jesus is restoring Peter to a place of service. But just as important, he wants to make sure Peter realizes what love for him is all about. It is caring for, feeding, shepherding—otherwise known as *loving*—the sheep. And that kind of love brings with it the possibility for and probability of pain. When was the last time you extended your heart to someone or something and had it trampled?
• Have you gotten the "love-wind" back in your sails, or is your boat still docked in the harbor?

- Respond to this statement: "The only place outside Heaven where you can be perfectly safe from all the dangers and perturbations of love is Hell."

READ

From *The Velveteen Rabbit*, by Margery Williams[4]

"Real isn't how you are made," said the Skin Horse. "It's a thing that happens to you. When a child loves you for a long, long time; not just to play with, but REALLY loves you, then you become Real."

"Does it hurt?" asked the Rabbit.

"Sometimes," said the Skin Horse, for he was always truthful. "When you are Real you don't mind being hurt."

"Does it happen all at once, like being wound up," he asked, "or bit by bit?"

"It doesn't happen all at once," said the Skin Horse. "You become. It takes a long time. That's why it doesn't often happen to people who break easily, or have sharp edges, or who have to be carefully kept. Generally, by the time you are Real, most of your hair has been loved off, and your eyes drop out and you get loose in the joints and very shabby. But these things don't matter at all, because once you are Real you can't be ugly, except to people who don't understand."

THINK   "Do you love me?"

- How does this promo for the Christian life sound to you: "Come have most of your hair loved off, lose your eyes, get real loose in your joints, and end up completely shabby!"?
- Is that the message you hear from most churches, pastors, and small groups?
- Listen again to the question "Do you love me?" Can you hear Jesus asking you? Remember, once you're really his, you can never be ugly, "except to people who don't understand."

THINK (continued)

PRAY

Look back at the "Think" sections. Ruminate on your responses.
Let them distill into a prayer, and then write that prayer below.

Yes, Lord, you know I love you . . .

The issue of prayer is not prayer; the issue of prayer is God.

Abraham Heschel

LIVE   "Do you love me?"

The challenge now is to take this question further along—to live out this question. Think of one thing, *just one*, that you can personally do to wrestle with the question, inhabit the character of it, and live it in everyday life. In the following space, jot down your thoughts on this "one thing." Read the Scripture and quotes that follow for additional inspiration. During the coming week, pray about this "one thing," talk with a close friend about it, and learn to live the question.

One thing . . .

The whole point of what we're urging is simply *love*—love uncontaminated by self-interest and counterfeit faith, a life open to God.

1 Timothy 1:5

This much is certain, that we have no theological right to set any sort of limits to the lovingkindness of God which has appeared in Jesus Christ.

Karl Barth, *The Humanity of God*

Live the questions now. Perhaps you will then gradually, without noticing it, live along some distant day into the answer.

RAINER MARIA RILKE, *LETTERS TO A YOUNG POET*

NOTES

LESSON 1

1. Madeleine L'Engle, *Walking on Water: Reflections on Faith and Art* (New York: Crosswicks, 1980), 54.
2. Gilbert K. Chesterton, *Orthodoxy* (New York: Doubleday, 1959), 49–51.
3. Kathleen Norris, *Amazing Grace: A Vocabulary of Faith* (New York: Riverhead Books, 1998), 62–63.
4. Walter Wangerin Jr., *The Orphean Passages: The Drama of Faith* (Grand Rapids, MI: Zondervan, 1996), 36–39.
5. Anne Lamott, *Traveling Mercies: Some Thoughts on Faith* (New York: Pantheon Books, 1999), 47–50.

LESSON 2

1. Barry Holstun Lopez, *Of Wolves and Men* (New York: Charles Scribner's Sons, 1978), 283–284.
2. Walter Brueggemann, *Living Toward a Vision: Biblical Reflections on Shalom* (New York: United Church Press, 1987), 167–171.
3. Wendell Berry, *The Memory of Old Jack* (New York: Harcourt, 1974), 76–78.

LESSON 3

1. Madeleine L'Engle, *Walking on Water: Reflections on Faith and Art* (Wheaton, IL: Harold Shaw Publishers, 1980), 98–104.
2. Fyodor Dostoevsky, *The Brothers Karamazov*, in *Shadow and Light: Literature and the Life of Faith*, ed. Darryl L. Tippens,

Stephen R. Weathers, and Jack Welch (Abilene, TX: ACU Press, 1997), 106–114.

LESSON 4

1. Ken Gire, *Intimate Moments with the Savior: Learning to Love* (Grand Rapids, MI: Zondervan, 1989), 55–58.
2. Larry Crabb, *The Safest Place on Earth* (Nashville: Word, 1999), 32.
3. Brennan Manning, *Abba's Child: The Cry of the Heart for Intimate Belonging* (Colorado Springs, CO: NavPress, 2002), 67–68.
4. Donald Gray, *Jesus—The Way to Freedom* (Winona, MN: St. Mary's College Press, 1979), 70, quoted in Brennan Manning, *Abba's Child: The Cry of the Heart for Intimate Belonging* (Colorado Springs, CO: NavPress, 2002), 67.

LESSON 5

1. Jerry Bridges, *The Pursuit of Holiness (25th Anniversary Edition)* (Colorado Springs, CO: NavPress, 2003), 56–57.
2. C. S. Lewis, *Mere Christianity* (New York: HarperCollins, 2001), p. 52.
3. http://www.simpleliving.org/catalog/FullText/WatchForLight .html#Authors.

LESSON 6

1. John Eldredge, *Waking the Dead: The Glory of a Heart Fully Alive* (Nashville: Thomas Nelson, 2003), 10–12.
2. Dallas Willard, *The Divine Conspiracy: Rediscovering Our Hidden Life in God* (San Francisco: HarperSanFrancisco, 1998), 38.
3. Philip Yancey, *The Jesus I Never Knew* (Grand Rapids, MI: Zondervan, 1995), 178–179.
4. Brennan Manning, *Abba's Child: The Cry of the Heart for Intimate Belonging* (Colorado Springs, CO: NavPress, 2002), 99–100.
5. H. A. Williams, *True Resurrection* (London: Mitchell Begley Limited, 1972), 5, quoted in Brennan Manning, *Abba's Child: The Cry of the Heart for Intimate Belonging* (Colorado Springs, CO: NavPress, 2002), 99.
6. Williams, 5.

7. William Barry, *God's Passionate Desire and Our Response* (Notre Dame, IN: Ave Maria Press, 1993), 109, quoted in Brennan Manning, *Abba's Child: The Cry of the Heart for Intimate Belonging* (Colorado Springs, CO: NavPress, 2002), 100.

LESSON 7

1. Alice Walker, "The Welcome Table," *In Love & Trouble: Stories of Black Women* (New York: Harcourt, 1974), 81–86.
2. Walter Wangerin Jr., *Ragman and Other Cries of Faith* (San Francisco: HarperSanFrancisco, 1984), 80–82.
3. Marge Piercy, *To Be of Use*, in *Good Poems*, ed. Garrison Keillor (New York: Penguin Books, 2002), 157.

LESSON 8

1. Sue Monk Kidd, *When the Heart Waits: Spiritual Direction for Life's Sacred Questions* (San Francisco: HarperSanFrancisco, 1990), 7–8.
2. Brennan Manning, *The Ragamuffin Gospel* (Sisters, OR: Multnomah, 1990), 159.
3. Walter Wangerin Jr., *Reliving the Passion: Meditations on the Suffering, Death, and Resurrection of Jesus as Recorded in Mark* (Grand Rapids, MI: Zondervan, 1992), 98–100.
4. T. S. Eliot, *Journey of the Magi*, in *Collected Poems 1909-1962* (New York: Harcourt, 1936), 99–100.

LESSON 9

1. Frederick Buechner, *Telling Secrets: A Memoir* (New York: HarperCollins, 1991), 7–10.
2. David Whyte, *The Heart Aroused: Poetry and the Preservation of the Soul in Corporate America* (New York: Bantam, Dell, Doubleday, 1994), 120, 124–125.
3. Carol Pearson, *The Hero Within: Six Archetypes We Live By* (San Francisco: Harper & Row, 1986), 129.
4. Madeleine L'Engle, *Walking on Water: Reflections on Faith and Art* (Wheaton, IL: Harold Shaw Publishers, 1980), 70–71.

5. Gerald G. May, MD, *The Awakened Heart: Opening Yourself to the Love You Need* (San Francisco: HarperSanFrancisco, 1991), 48–49.

LESSON 10

1. Ken Gire, *Intimate Moments with the Savior: Learning to Love* (Grand Rapids, MI: Zondervan, 1989), 140–141.
2. Michael Card, "Stranger on the Shore," *Immanuel: Reflections on the Life of Christ* (Nashville: Thomas Nelson, 1990), 195.
3. C. S. Lewis, *The Four Loves: The Much Beloved Exploration of the Nature of Love* (New York: Harcourt, 1960), 120–121.
4. Margery Williams, *The Velveteen Rabbit*, in *A Call to Character: A Family Treasury of Stories, Poems, Plays, Proverbs, and Fables to Guide the Development of Values for You and Your Children*, ed. Colin Greer and Herbert Kohl (New York: HarperCollins, 1995), 413.

GROW STRONGER IN YOUR FAITH
BY WRESTLING WITH
LIFE'S BIGGEST QUESTIONS.

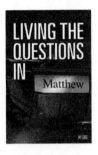

Living the Questions in Matthew
1-57683-833-1

Many believers think of Jesus as the man with all the answers, sent down to earth to tell us everything we need to know. So why are we still left with so many nagging questions we never seem to find answers for?

Now readers and study groups can consider some of the major questions Jesus posed to his followers. This fresh new study of the gospel of Matthew, using *The Message*—the eye-opening translation by Eugene Peterson—will help readers embrace life's questions and build a stronger faith in the process.

Visit your local Christian bookstore,
call NavPress at 1-800-366-7788, or log on to www.navpress.com
to purchase.

To locate a Christian bookstore near you, call 1-800-991-7747.

NAVPRESS ®
BRINGING TRUTH TO LIFE
w w w . n a v p r e s s . c o m